GRILLED
CHEESE

& Tasting Menus

GRILLED CHEESE

& Tasting Menus

Stories of Growth and Change

NICOLE HOLLAR

MINDSET PRESS, LLC

ISBN: 979-8-9883168-5-5 (Paperback)
ISBN: 979-8-9883168-6-2 (eBook)
Library of Congress Control Number: 2025913168
Published in Fort Lauderdale, FL

Editor: Katrina Nichols
Cover designer: Lori Pratico
Interior layout: Saqib

Visit the author's website for purchases, bookings, and workshops:

www.nicolehollar.com

Also by Nicole Hollar

FEELING STUCK?
Empower Yourself to Live a Happier,
More Fulfilling Life

LOGGED IN, CHECKED OUT
Boost Productivity and Improve
Communication

To knowing that comfort isn't the same as fulfillment, and you don't have to settle for just being full.

TABLE OF CONTENTS

WELCOME TO THE TABLE   1

1ˢᵗ COURSE   9

Too Smart   12

Comfort Food   15

Ice Cream   19

You Deserve More   21

Stretching   23

90/10   25

Abandoned   28

Fat Like Us   30

Thank You, Judy   32

2ⁿᵈ COURSE   35

Is There More?   39

Eye Roll   42

Towels   44

Road Trips   46

Bushes   48

Echo Chambers   50

Grandfather Clocks   55

Repent! (Just Kidding)   57

Loud   59

Cards We Hide Behind   62

Pick Up the Phone!   66

Belonging   68

Voice   70

Identity   72

3rd COURSE   **77**

Sex Ed   80

What About Me?   83

Pianos & Presents   85

Hairy Subjects   88

Portals   91

Divorce   93

Blockbuster Night   96

Good Wine   98

4th COURSE   **103**

Metabolife   106

Open Road   111

Don't Be Weird About It   113

Spicy & Sweet   115

Unraveled   118

Awkward   121

Capable   123

5th COURSE   **129**

Diversity   131

Disconnected Connection   133

How Was School?   136

F*@k Gail!   138

Effort   141

Dance Floor   145

CHECK, PLEASE   **147**

GRILLED CHEESE MENU   **149**

ACKNOWLEDGEMENTS   **153**

ABOUT THE AUTHOR   **155**

WELCOME TO THE TABLE

It's funny how some memories stick with you, isn't it? Some are exciting, like getting your first puppy. Others seem random but might teach you something about yourself or other people; like the time I wore a leather biker jacket to school, and my 12th grade physics lab partner—someone I usually got along with well—suddenly treated me like I was a stranger. When I asked her if she was acting differently because of what I was wearing, she froze. It was a moment that struck me. Same person, different jacket. It was a reminder of how quickly people judge based on appearances, even people who should know better.

Other memories are fleeting, a moment in time captured without any discernible impact. Then there are those times of clarity or fear; experiences that force you to learn. But out of all the memories we carry, some stand out simply because they feel warm. They don't change the trajectory of your life, but they wrap you up in a moment of comfort, making you feel safe and whole. For me, that warm memory is grilled cheese.

It's the sound of flimsy, sticky cheese being unwrapped from its plastic, waiting to be transformed. I'll be honest, I never liked American cheese straight from the wrapper. As a kid, my face would contort in disgust when I watched friends pull out a slice from the fridge to snack on after school. But that same cheese grilled between two slices of buttery bread was delicious!

I can still hear the butter sizzling, crackling, and popping as little golden droplets skittered across the pan's surface, waiting for the sandwich to join them. The smell of toasty bread turning crisp instantly takes me back to my family kitchen. I'd stand on a chair so I could watch the Italian bread transform into something golden and crunchy as the cheese melted into gooey perfection.

For me, grilled cheese wasn't just a sandwich. It was warmth. It was love folded between two buttery slices of bread. I still joke that my favorite food is bread and butter. That kind of simplicity, that kind of consistency, is what childhood memories are made of.

Grilled cheese was also one of the first meals I ever learned to cook. I started by buttering the bread. Then, under Mom's watchful eye, I graduated to flipping the sandwich in the pan. Eventually, I took over the whole process. Before I was in double digits, grilled cheese was my specialty, something I could make for my family that made me feel proud.

Even decades later, just the thought of a grilled cheese sandwich feels like being wrapped up in a cozy blanket on a cold day. I bet you have a memory like that, too, something that reminds you of a time when the world felt a little less complicated. Whatever it is, those memories have a way of pulling us back, even for just a moment, to a place where things felt easy and safe.

But there comes a time when grilled cheese isn't enough, and you start to wonder what else is out there. As much as we love its comfort, we become curious and eventually start to crave something more. Over the decades my curiosity taught me to be a creative cook who can make a reasonably healthy and balanced meal from whatever is in the fridge; a skill appreciated by my wife, Jeana, who makes an excellent turkey meatloaf, and exceptional reservations.

Eventually, if you allow it, you might step out of your comfort zone entirely and try something new—like Thai or Vietnamese food, Dim Sum, or Middle Eastern cuisine. Or reach a point in life when dining becomes more than food; it becomes a unique and creative experience shared by the guests, service staff, and the chef—a tasting menu.

The first time I sat down for a tasting menu was with Jeana, an adventurous foodie. I'll admit I was a bit suspicious and did some web browsing to understand much of what I was reading. There were dishes with descriptions I had to look up and ingredients I'd never heard of. Words like "gastrique," "umami," and "amuse-bouche" suddenly entered my vocabulary. Each plate was like a tiny work of art, with layers of flavors and textures arranged with precision. It wasn't just food; it was an experience. It wasn't safe or predictable, but it was exciting. It pushed me to stay curious, to try something new, even if I wasn't sure I'd like it.

A true tasting menu isn't just a series of random dishes. It's curated. A chef carefully designs the journey, with each course building on the last with palette cleansers to prepare your taste buds for the next dish. Flavors dance together, balancing sweetness with spice, crunch with creaminess. It's enough to satisfy but not overwhelm. It's a bit like life—*knowing how to appreciate its complexity while knowing when to slow down.* It reminds us that even as we explore the new, there's always a place for something simple, something like grilled cheese. It's also a reminder that *curiosity opens the door to learning something new and that it's perfectly okay to decide it's not for you.*

∞

While I've always been curious, I wish I could say I've always embraced change. But the truth is, I used to cling to the familiar and the path I imagined for myself. I thought I had figured everything out when I was young: I'd go to high school, then college, get my MBA, and by twenty-three I'd be married, with four kids by the time I was thirty. That was the plan. I even tattooed my vision of success in business as a tramp stamp on my lower back—because nothing says #lifegoals like a tattoo you can't see without a mirror.

Then I learned that life isn't scripted or linear. It zigs and zags. It takes you places you didn't expect to go, and sometimes, it forces you to cleanse your palette and let go of what you thought you wanted. Sometimes it drops you right into the middle of the unknown. Like when I packed up and moved to Miami, unemployed with middle management goals, and no plan other than wanting to speak Spanish more often.

I'd studied Spanish from middle school through college, and even spent a semester in Venezuela, but I wasn't using the language. It felt like a perishable skill that was slipping away. So, at twenty-five years old, I jumped and left behind everything that felt familiar. It wasn't an easy decision. My grandpa had passed away not long before, and my grandma, who I was very close to, was living alone. Leaving felt selfish, like I was abandoning her. But she had my mom, my aunt, and my uncle around her, so I had to trust she'd be okay.

Not long after I made the decision to move to Florida my mom moved in with my grandma after a fire destroyed my mother's house. I felt better knowing that Grandma wouldn't be alone. That gave me the "permission" I needed to go. Moving 1000 miles from home taught me a few things I didn't expect: you must create space in your life to make room for something new; how to roll with life's punches; and when to let go.

Life is not a straight line from grilled cheese to tasting menus. It's a winding road full of twists and turns, with plenty of detours along the way. I didn't find the middle-management job I'd hoped for. Instead, I worked as a server on South Beach, proofread catalogs, transcribed television shows, worked as a model scout, and even took my hard-earned MBA off my resume because employers thought it made me overqualified. It was humbling, frustrating, and at times, humiliating. But it also forced me to adapt. While the move looked nothing like I'd planned, it turned out to be exactly what I needed. I let go of the rigid expectations I'd placed on myself and started to *see life as a series of choices rather than a checklist.*

Eventually, the landlord of my studio apartment told me he could probably get me a part-time job as a personal trainer at the gym where he worked. Since mainstream gym personal trainers were a newer fad, they hired pretty much anyone. Lucky me. With zero knowledge or experience, I got the job. I worked at a restaurant several nights per week and at the gym. Despite no fitness experience other than working out myself, or training on how to sell fitness packages, my boss would frequently ask me what my sales were for the month. Well, zero, of course.

I was scraping by on minimum wage showing people how to use gym equipment. There were moments when I didn't know how I'd pay the rent. I'd budget groceries down to the last dollar and write checks I hoped wouldn't clear until after payday. Though I knew I could go *home* I came very close to deciding to sleep in my car and put my belongings in storage instead. It was hard, but it taught me how to hustle and adapt. I saw it as a problem to solve.

A few months after I started working at the gym, one of my coworkers, who had taken me under her wing, was promoted to personal training director at another club. She asked me to transfer with her as her assistant, and I did. I learned a lot from Seven. She was affable and genuinely invested in developing her staff. That focus on staff development became a core principle for me when I took over as training director at the same club when Seven left.

At that time, the company had implemented a week-long onboarding program for all new trainers, which reinforced the importance of investing time in your people. Within a year, I moved and transferred to a club near me, stepping back into a trainer role under a director I respected. Unfortunately, after a couple of years the focus moved away from staff development and client nurturing, and back to chasing revenue, making it clear that the people-first culture I thrived in was changing.

One Sunday morning, I found myself crying in bed, looking at my then-partner, saying, "Don't make me go back there." That was the moment I knew I needed to leave. I loved my clients and what I did, but the environment was killing my soul. I didn't have a clear plan, but just as I had years earlier, I trusted myself to figure it out. Within six months I left with three clients and started training them in my 12'x12' living room. It wasn't glamorous, but it was mine.

I had to trust in my ability to figure it out. I've worn so many hats I've lost count, and I've learned it's about showing up, even when you're scared and you have no idea what you are doing. It's about learning to pronounce "quinoa" correctly and realizing that beef carpaccio is a fancy way of saying raw, thin sliced meat—and trying it anyway even if you're not sure you'll like it. It's about trusting that you'll find your way somehow. *Growth is messy, uncomfortable, and rarely feels like progress in the moment. It's awkward, and half the time, you don't even realize it's happening. But it's also where we learn who we are. It's where we figure out what to hold onto and what to let go of.*

∞

And growth isn't just about moving forward, it's also about looking back—about understanding the habits, patterns, and memories that shaped us. For me, that means thinking about my family. My grandparents, my mom, my extended family. They all taught me something about connection, about love, and about how messy relationships can be. My grandma wasn't the touchy-feely type, but I taught her to hug me and tell me she loved me. I still remember the day my mom almost fainted when my grandma said, "Bye, honey," as I left the house. Moments like that remind me that growth isn't just about you; it's about how you show up for the people around you, too.

I credit my childhood for my resilience. As an only child people often assume I was spoiled and had all the attention. When in reality, I had to share if I wanted play friends, learn to initiate if I wanted attention, and figure out how to keep myself busy. My family—my mom, maternal grandparents, aunt and uncle—wasn't perfect. There was a lot of love, but there was also dysfunction, jealousy, and some toxic patterns. I grew up surrounded by people who didn't always know how to communicate or set boundaries, and for a long time, I carried those patterns with me. It wasn't until I started doing the real work—therapy, reflection, choosing my own path—that I realized I didn't have to hold onto those behaviors. I could choose something different.

Now, I look at my life and see how far I've come. I didn't marry at twenty-three or have four kids by thirty, but I did find my person, my wonderful wife, Jeana, and together we've built a life I'm proud of. We have fur kids, our home, and a lot of love and respect. And while life isn't always easy, I've learned that I get to choose how I navigate it. I get to decide what to hold onto and what to let go of. And that, more than anything, is what makes life so beautiful.

1ˢᵀ COURSE

Grilled cheese offers comfort—the kind we often seek when life feels uncertain. But the truth is, not everything that once comforted us continues to serve us as we grow. The sandwich that felt like love and warmth at eight years old might leave us wanting something more substantial as adults. It represents the habits and beliefs we cling to, the ones that used to provide a sense of safety or belonging but no longer nourish us in the way we need. Our unconscious holds onto these comforts, often pulling us back to old ways, even when we've outgrown them.

Our lives are full of these subtle, often unquestioned patterns. Sometimes, those scripts in our heads are clear as day. Things we repeat because they've been baked into us over time: "This is how I've always done it," or "My family always said..." Other times, they run quietly in the background, influencing decisions without our awareness. It begs the question: how much of what we carry today is a choice, and how much is simply a leftover from years ago?

The way our unconscious minds protect us is a concept that has fascinated me for quite a while. It holds onto patterns that were once useful, even if now they feel outdated. It's as if our minds have their own well-stocked pantry of beliefs, keeping them there for safekeeping, even when we've evolved past them. That pantry doesn't care whether the beliefs are empowering or limiting. It holds onto everything. And because the unconscious is always trying to keep us safe, it can make stepping into new territory feel impossibly risky. Even if we're craving something new, we might find ourselves reaching for plain bread—familiar but unsatisfying.

This isn't just a mental game; our bodies store these patterns too. We tense up, brace ourselves, or change our posture as if to protect ourselves from threats that aren't even there anymore. It's like our nervous systems remember the discomfort, the fear, or the embarrassment we once felt, and they react to keep us safe. We carry those memories in our muscles, our fascia, our breathing, and our very being, long after the moment has passed. It's a well-meaning but outdated form of self-protection.

Sometimes, we get so caught up in the small wins—the things that make us feel momentarily good—that we don't notice we're still craving something deeper. Sometimes it's like eating ice cream when we are at an emotional low. The physical pleasure masking the emotional pain for just a moment. We tell ourselves we're fine, that change isn't necessary, even when we're craving more. We focus on what's easy and comfortable, even when the nourishment we really need requires a little more effort, and a little more vulnerability. It's not always easy to admit when we're leaning on something outdated, but recognizing those patterns is the first step to moving beyond them.

There's a certain grace in giving ourselves permission to let go of comforts that no longer serve us. Some beliefs, routines, or coping mechanisms we've inherited aren't even ours to keep. They're "family recipes" passed down from generation to generation. Ideas about worth, happiness, or success get passed down too, influencing what we think is possible. But just because they've always been there doesn't mean we have to keep them. We have the choice to rewrite those recipes, to create something more aligned with our current needs.

What would it look like to question those old comforts? To keep what still fits and let go of what doesn't? It's not about throwing everything away but about being discerning. Some things are worth holding onto, but others have outlived their purpose. When we make the choice to examine our habits, beliefs, and routines, we make space for something new. We give ourselves permission to step forward and evolve.

Life keeps moving, whether we're ready or not. It's full of interactions and experiences that invite us to grow, challenge our comfort zones, or ask us to reconsider what we thought we knew. Growth, I've learned, isn't about having all the answers; it's about staying curious and being willing to ask questions. It's about *savoring the moments that truly matter and being brave enough to let go of the rest.*

So, here's to grilled cheese. To the comfort it once gave, to the joy of nostalgia, and to the courage of letting it be a fond memory instead of a daily crutch. Here's to exploring what else is on the menu, to savoring the new flavors that come with growth, and to understanding that sometimes, *moving forward means making peace with what we leave behind.*

Too Smart

"I guess she's too smart for the family business." "It's tough out there." These were the phrases my client Rachel heard over and over when she graduated college. She knew they weren't true, but they held her back. Rachel hovered between the positions of executive director and vice president for years. No matter what she did, something always got in the way of her reaching the vice president role.

Rachel was stuck. She came to me for one-to-one Mindset Transformation Coaching®, a process where I lead people to release limiting beliefs and obstacles at an unconscious level and provide them with new, more effective tools that facilitate progress and fulfillment. We started with a deep dive into her habits, beliefs, and values. Rachel and I went through her daily routines, her career history, her family background, and even her deepest fears and aspirations.

As we talked, Rachel shared stories about her upbringing. Her family had always been very close-knit, and they had a small family business that everyone joined. Rachel, however, had ambitions beyond the family business and wanted to sample life on her own path. She went to college, got her degree, and started climbing the corporate ladder. Despite her success, her family's words taunted her each time she reached for a new rung on the corporate ladder.

I explained to Rachel that she was holding onto learned guilt, the kind of guilt that someone passive-aggressively installs, or directly tells you that you should feel badly about. "I can't believe you took the last cookie. How selfish," is learned guilt. This is different than inherent guilt which is internal and intended to teach. For example, if you step on a dog's paw and it hurts him, you are likely to feel bad. That does not mean you should punish yourself forever, it means that perhaps you need to look behind you when you take a step in the kitchen, figuring the dog might be waiting for fallen treats.

During our sessions, we uncovered that Rachel felt guilty about her success because she felt as though she was snubbing her family. Her family had been wholly committed to their business and made a modest, stable life for themselves. They lived a simple grilled cheese lifestyle. She believed that if she reached the top, she'd be metaphorically rubbing her success in their faces, proving that she was smarter, and that didn't sit well with her.

We delved deeper into her childhood and how her perception of family expectations shaped her beliefs, then we reframed them. I asked Rachel to think about what her success really meant. Did it really mean she was betraying or snubbing her family? Or could it be that she was honoring her family by embracing their work ethic and commitment? What if her success was a testament to the values they had instilled in her?

Though Rachel had unconsciously embedded those post-college phrases in her mind, we did an exercise to help her uncover some other memories that did not surface as frequently. Rachel remembered her father's proud smile when she graduated from university and the way her mother would brag about her to the neighbors. These memories helped Rachel reframe her success as something her family was proud of, rather than something they resented. Then I asked Rachel, "Is it possible that the comment about being too smart was actually your dad's way of commenting that you are intelligent, that he knows you will reach higher than what the business could offer you, and that he'll miss you?"

We had just finished the memory recall exercise and Rachel just stared at me blankly. "I guess it is," she muttered. "Not everyone uses words well, Rachel, so we interpret them however we want to," I replied. "Your dad, who you said was not overly emotional, probably doesn't even remember saying that."

Rachel started to see things differently. She realized that she had not abandoned her family. Instead, her guilt was hiding her fear of success and what it meant for her. Once we eliminated that limiting belief, she was able to accept that it was possible to achieve great things without losing touch with where you came from.

Rachel let go of her guilt and hidden fear and things started to change. She became more confident in her abilities and started to act as a vice president, advocating for herself and her vision. She no longer saw obstacles as roadblocks but as challenges to overcome. Her attitude shift didn't go unnoticed. She was promoted to vice president within the year.

What about you? Have you ever felt guilty about your achievements? Being successful because you work hard is not a betrayal, and you can reach for your dreams without feeling bad about it. Imagine what it would be like to let go of any guilt or fear and fully embrace your potential.

Comfort Food

B rian, a fitness client, was very clearly frustrated after doing a routine measurement check-in. "I'm doing all the things I'm supposed to be doing, but it still feels like a struggle. When does it get easier?" he blustered.

He was impatient, he wanted results, and he wanted them now. I understood. We live in a world that celebrates quick fixes, next-day shipping, and overnight transformations, and the idea of slow, steady progress can feel maddening.

I met his gaze, his eyes swirling with irritation. "You're not alone in this," I assured him, "It's not about willpower or discipline alone; it's about where you are in the process of making change second nature."

"Think of it like learning to walk. You didn't know what you didn't know. In the beginning, you didn't even know walking was a thing. You were content crawling. That's where you used to be with your habits. You didn't realize how your food habits and choices affected your body. You didn't know that you didn't know."

It's a phase called *unconscious incompetence,* the first of the Four Stages of Competence, a learning model referenced in psychology that describes the phases people must go through to create long-term change.

I continued. "Remember when you knew your habits needed to change, but you weren't sure how?" That's the tough part—recognizing a problem but feeling powerless to fix it. That is the next stage—*conscious incompetence.*

That's when Brian reached out for help.

"You've made progress since then wouldn't you agree?" I asked. He shrugged in modest agreement. "Right now, you're in that stage where every choice feels deliberate and exhausting. You have to think about skipping the chips or opting for water instead of soda, and it feels like work and deprivation."

I reminded him of the process of making long-term changes and that he was now in the *conscious competence* stage. Each day Brian had to make conscious choices that aligned with his goals.

Just like driving or tying your shoes, good habits become automatic. I reminded Brian that with enough conscious repetition, he would reach a point where it doesn't even occur to him to browse the cookie aisle unless he genuinely wanted one.

I assured him that it would get easier. "Your unconscious mind is powerful. Right now, it's holding onto old routines that feel comfortable, even if they don't serve you. But with time and practice, it'll learn new ones."

And that's the thing about building habits; repetition is not glamorous or exciting. It's making choices that feel uncomfortable or even pointless at first, trusting that the effort will pay off in the long run. It's choosing a salad when you're craving fries. It feels like a compromise in the beginning. But as Brian discovered, over time, your taste for what's good for you develops, and you start craving the things that genuinely nourish you.

Our unconscious mind loves routine. It clings to familiar patterns like making grilled cheese even when you want to lose weight. It doesn't care if the habit is beneficial or harmful; it just repeats what it knows is efficient or seems safe. With Neuro-Linguistic Programming (NLP) and Mental and Emotional Release® (MER), tools that I use in coaching, scratching and replacing ineffective patterns in the unconscious is instantaneous. NLP and MER are psycho-behavioral methods that address thoughts, language, and experience, and how they relate to behavior. We use them to release limiting beliefs and obstacles and reframe how the unconscious creates meaning and behaviors to create positive change based on effective modeling behavior.

However, even without those tools you can rewire those deep-seated patterns with consistent, intentional effort, and that's what Brian had been doing all along. He was teaching his conscious mind something new, even if the rewards weren't immediate.

Then came the day when Brian walked into my office looking different, lighter somehow. With a small, proud smile, he looked at me and said, "You won't believe what happened this morning," excitement bubbling over. "I got up, drank a glass of water, and went for a walk. I didn't even have to think about it. It just happened."

I couldn't help but smile back at him. "See? That's the shift. You're moving into the final stage we talked about, *unconscious competence.* The choices that used to feel forced are starting to come naturally."

We both remembered the days when every step felt uphill, when Brian had to battle with himself just to follow through on the smallest commitment. But now, his unconscious mind was on board, making decisions that aligned with his goals without resistance. He was a far cry from where he'd started, a place where his habits were dragging him down.

It hadn't been an easy road. Change rarely is. But Brian's journey was a testament to the power of patience and persistence. Each conscious decision he made, no matter how small, had built a foundation for something greater. His old routines didn't disappear overnight, but with time, they faded, making way for habits that truly served him.

We all have our own versions of comfort food—those habits or beliefs that make us feel safe but keep us from growing. The trick is to notice when we're leaning on them out of habit and gently guide ourselves toward choices that serve us better. *It's not about being perfect or expecting everything to change at once. It's about building a life where good decisions come easily, and where we're not fighting ourselves every step of the way.*

While most change isn't instantaneous, it's absolutely possible. The journey to unconscious competence is worth every awkward, uncomfortable step. Because one day, the things that once felt like a battle will feel as natural as breathing. And when that happens, life starts to feel a little lighter, a little easier, and a whole lot more aligned.

Ice Cream

My cousin Noelle, who feels more like a sister to me, is almost nine years younger. The day she was born was an exciting day for me. Unlike many cousins, we spent a lot of time together at our grandparents' home when she was very young, and I often babysat her.

As a toddler Noelle would sit on my back while I lay on my belly, brushing my hair with the back of the hairbrush and occasionally the bristles. We watched TV together, though not in a conventional way, of course, but with me lying on my back with my legs to the ceiling, and tiny Noelle perched on my feet.

I'd often drag her around the yard and sometimes up the sidewalk in a Radio Flyer® wagon hitched to the riding lawn mower. Don't worry, the blades weren't down! It was the 1980s, a different time when we still played with lawn darts.

Despite our age difference, like siblings, we had our fair share of pestering and tormenting each other. Being much younger, Noelle's antics were mainly physical, like jumping off the sofa onto me while I napped on the floor. I, on the other hand, took advantage of her gullibility.

In fact, one incident that we still laugh about today happened when Noelle was about the age of six. I saw her eating a bowl of Oreo® ice cream and convinced her that the little dark pieces in the ice cream were ants, and the only way to kill them was to eat salt. There she stood, in the kitchen with a palm full of table salt, reluctantly dabbing her tongue into the small mound and causing a great deal of commotion. My grandma heard the ruckus and swooped around the corner, rushing into the kitchen and yelling at her to stop.

As the instigator, I slipped away from the scene quickly. Despite the playful intent, Noelle jokes that its trauma is responsible for her healthy disinterest in ice cream and a preference for low-salt foods.

It's a reminder that our perception of harmless teasing can have a lasting impact on others. We never know how our actions and words can shape someone's preferences and behaviors in unexpected ways.

You Deserve More

I once told Sarah, a coaching client, "You deserve more than what your parents showed you." She instantly burst into tears and asked, "Why would you say that?" We had been discussing her parents' severe health problems and her struggle to break free from their unhealthy patterns. Despite knowing how detrimental their lifestyle was, she couldn't help following in their footsteps like a moth to a flame.

She joined fitness programs, tried different diets, and went to retreats. But after a while she found herself slipping back into old habits. When we explored Sarah's childhood memories, she recounted how her parents would often indulge in unhealthy foods and sedentary activities. Her mom would make her father unhealthy food to keep him happy while simultaneously being frustrated at her husband's weight and medical problems, all while battling her own health issues. Even with advanced diabetes, neuropathy, excess weight, and limited mobility, her dad still left the house each day for donuts. She loved them dearly, but their collective lifestyles were taking a toll on her.

Sarah didn't know it beforehand, but when I made that deliberate statement, I hit a trigger: she unconsciously felt that being healthier and demanding it when she visited her parents was a betrayal and an act of insubordination to them. Yet, it wasn't. It was about recognizing her own worth and potential. It wasn't about rejecting or defying her parents; it was about honoring herself.

During our coaching sessions, we worked on reshaping Sarah's beliefs and boundaries. Together we worked on detaching her emotions from her eating habits, improving her self-worth, and taught her how to stand by her needs when visiting her family rather than shifting back into a subordinate childlike role. Though she could stand up for her needs to friends, it was harder with authority figures like parents. I reminded her that if they wanted her to be happy as she said they did, often making her childhood food favorites when she visited, then they would modify their behavior to reflect her current needs. If they were unwilling, then it was never about her, it was about them.

The unconscious mind toys with us, playing in the background and running 95% of our life, even if the recording no longer serves us. With time, focus, and repetition you can help reshape your beliefs and needs to meet your present-day self with conscious creation. But it all starts with recognizing that *you are deserving and worthy of love, joy, success, abundance, and fulfillment without guilt.*

What would it mean for you to seek happiness and fulfillment without feeling bad for others? Your journey is uniquely yours, and it's okay to honor it with pride and joy to become the best version of yourself. Give yourself permission to become the tasting menu—full of layers, flavors and new experiences.

Stretching

In my world of fitness, the customary way I begin working with a client is they reach out to me, we have a brief exchange via email or phone, then we set up a consultation. Depending on your age you might remember Barbara Walters and her interview style. Often, her guest would cry at some point. I was once nicknamed Barbara by co-workers.

Now, not everyone sheds tears during a consultation, but I guess you would say that I am not afraid of other people showing emotion so sometimes it leaks out, even during a consultation. But, even if words don't reveal personal information, the body might.

I imagine you've been around someone who is having a hard day, and while they said nothing, you could feel it in their body language and energy. I've made a career out of reading body language, observing how words are used, noticing where people have physical challenges or limitations, and feeling how a person responds to touch and discomfort. This is how my career naturally evolved from only fitness into personal development and growth coaching as well.

On one occasion, after the very first training session with a new client who I knew very little about, I took a leap and asked her who was violent in her home. Without hesitation, she said her dad was. I asked if she wanted to tell me more and she gave me a brief summary of what that looked like for her. Then she paused, looked at me puzzled both by the fact that I asked her out of nowhere, and that she responded so willingly. You see, I knew she was fueled by anxiety—oftentimes a long-held response to unspecified fear due to trauma someone experienced, or the absence of love, attention, and affection as a child.

During the moment I asked her, we were doing a partner-assisted hamstring stretch where the person lies on their back and the partner lifts a single leg towards the ceiling. Sure, she had somewhat tight hamstrings, but her body responded to my stretch with signs of fear, not general discomfort. Her body tensed in a way you might when hearing a fight, and her shoulders shrugged like they might if one was ducking or cowering.

Our bodies are always telling us something. Listen.

90/10

Anette, a fitness client who had weight loss frustration similar to Brian, came to me with her own challenges and unique twists. "I stay away from junk food for longer periods now," she told me one day. "I only fall off the wagon for a couple of weeks."

"That's part of your problem, Anette," I replied, not one to sugarcoat the truth. "You keep telling yourself that you're falling off, but the reality is that you're not usually on the wagon to begin with." I continued, "Your mind is telling you that you're focused on your goals when, in reality, you're mostly off course. Until you accept where you truly are, you're giving yourself a false sense of success—a way to avoid feeling bad because you think you should be doing better."

Anette spent about 90% of her time thinking about living a healthier lifestyle but only about 10% of her time acting on it. As long as she kept a fraction of her thoughts tied to the desire to become healthier then her mind believed any effort was the same. *The act of thinking about change, much like visualization techniques, can deceive the brain into believing it is making change.* But unlike an athlete visualizing a perfect throw which helps wire motor neurons, weight loss requires specific action. Anette was on a merry-go-round, believing that being 90% on target and 10% off was the same as being 90% off target with 10% progress because her thinking and doing had blended in her mind. She was deceiving herself.

Is there an area in your life where you might be telling yourself a similar story? A place where you think you're closer to your goals than you actually are. What would happen if you took an honest look at where you stand? What would happen if you stopped saying "I should," a phrase I suggested people abandon in my last book, *Feeling Stuck? Empower Yourself to Live a Happier, More Fulfilling Life* because it clutters the mind with false action and feelings of guilt.

The more time I spent working with clients like Anette, the more interested I became in understanding what keeps people stuck in these vicious cycles. That curiosity is what led me to develop Mindset Transformation Coaching®, the program and process I created to affect change at its highest level.

Many people have weight loss goals, and some of them have been my clients. They're often proud of their 30-pound weight loss—each time they lose it. The problem is that they keep gaining it back, as if trapped in an endless loop. They excitedly tell me, "Look, I got below 200 pounds!" But in the back of my mind, I'm wondering if this time will be different; if they'll continue moving closer to 180 pounds instead of creeping back above 200. Months pass, and I hear it again, "Look, I got below 200 pounds!" It's a cycle that keeps people stuck for years, even a lifetime.

It's not much different from having the same argument with your spouse over and over again, only to hear them say, "I understand. I'll do better." You sit there, hopeful that this time they mean it, only to find yourself in the same fight months later.

With sincerity in my voice, I looked at Anette and said, "You haven't let go of the unconscious emotional baggage that pulls you back to the familiar feeling of unhappiness. When you do, you'll become a new version of yourself."

Imagine if your habits truly supported the life you want to live. What habits have you genuinely created, and which ones are still in the making? Are you willing to do the work to turn conscious choices into unconscious habits that align with your goals?

For Anette, lasting change will only happen when she lets go of the emotional baggage that's holding her back—when she lets go of the "comfort cravings" her unconscious is wired to seek. That is when she'll keep moving forward instead of feeling the constant tug of her unconscious mind pulling her back above 200 pounds, back to a place of unhappiness that's become all too familiar.

Until she identifies and releases her underlying feelings of being un-lovable and unhappy, Anette's unconscious mind will keep pulling her back to feeling that way. With NLP and MER coaching techniques we can eradicate those feelings quickly, but without them, Anette can rewrite her programming if she stays focused and empowered long enough to make those unconscious changes.

Abandoned

H ave you ever wondered why certain words or events from your past still hold such power over you? It's wild how our childhood experiences shape our beliefs, sometimes in ways we don't even realize. It's why you might turn to tomato soup and a gooey cheese sandwich on a cold, crappy day.

Many years ago, my client Rosemary, a spirited woman, made a choice that so many in her generation faced: she left her home country, and came to the United States in search of a better life, leaving her young daughter with her mother. Today, the adult version of her daughter gets why her mother left. She understands the sacrifice. But that five-year-old girl? She felt abandoned. She didn't see the bigger picture; she just knew her mommy left her. I know this because I know her daughter. I hear it in her words and see it in her behaviors.

When I asked Rosemary if she had ever considered acknowledging what I believe to be her daughter's childhood feelings, she got defensive. "Have you ever thought about saying, 'I realize it must have been scary when you were a little girl not knowing why I left. I imagine you may have felt abandoned. I did it so we could both have a better life. Can you see that now?'"

Rosemary was insistent that she did nothing wrong. And you know what? That's true for her. She made a tough choice and did what she believed she needed to do for the benefit of her family. But the truth of a child is often different from the truth of an adult. And there is a child driving a part of all of us. What could change in their relationship if Rosemary simply acknowledged her daughter's core feelings?

My suggestion to Rosemary was not about right or wrong; it was about recognizing and validating the emotions of that young child still living within her daughter. *Sometimes, a simple act of empathy or reframing can scratch the old record playing in our unconscious mind, making room for healing and growth.*

Fat Like Us

I'll never forget Becky, a client who lost 50 pounds and was so excited to show her family during the holidays. She grew up in a family that never focused on health. They were all a bit overweight and not very active. After living away for 15 years, Becky forgot what it was like to be around them.

Becky's weight loss journey was inspiring. She started by making small changes on her own—swapping sugary drinks for water, adding more vegetables to her meals, and taking daily walks. Over time, those small changes added up. Becky began to feel more energetic and confident, eventually hiring me to help her get through a plateau.

When she got to her parents' house for Thanksgiving, her brother greeted her with, "I guess she doesn't want to be fat like us anymore." Her mom added, "She probably brought her own food because mine isn't good enough anymore." Becky told me all of this during a phone call while she was away. She was crushed. Her excitement vanished. She had expected support and encouragement but instead was met with sarcasm and judgment.

When she returned, we talked about that visit in our sessions. Becky described how she felt when her brother and mother made those comments. It was like all her hard work was being dismissed. She suddenly realized that she had felt guilty for wanting to be healthier, as if betraying her family's way of life. During our sessions, Becky realized one reason she never focused on her health was because of passive comments like these which she heard her family make about other people as she grew up.

Until she left home they were never directed at her because she was one of them. I explained to her that her family's remarks were about their own insecurities and the concept that "hurt people hurt people." Until Becky left home 15 years earlier, she took their comments to heart and felt guilty for even considering the idea of sampling something different. It was the time and space that gave her the room to want and pursue a healthier lifestyle menu.

Eventually, Becky let go of the guilt that had resurfaced at Thanksgiving. She realized that it was okay to pursue a healthier lifestyle, even if it meant being different from her family. Just because she wanted to change, it didn't mean she devalued their choices.

We worked on ways for Becky to navigate these family dynamics. I encouraged her to have an open conversation with her family about her goals and how their comments affected her, reminding them it was not a personal judgment about their lifestyle. It wasn't about asking for their approval but about setting boundaries and expressing her feelings.

The next holiday season, Becky approached things differently. She didn't hide her lifestyle changes or push them onto her family. Instead, she shared her journey and explained why it was important to her. Surprisingly, her family was more receptive. They even tried some of her healthy recipes and joined her for a walk after dinner.

If you've ever felt guilty for making positive changes, remember that *embracing your path doesn't diminish others*. It shows what's possible and gives them permission to grow, too.

Thank You, Judy

A couple of years into our relationship, my wife Jeana's parents came to our new home for a visit. Her mother Judy and I had some time alone to talk and were having good, genuine, heartfelt conversations. So, I asked her a question that had been on my mind: "Why did you believe that Jeana being gay was a curse from God?"

Jeana told me that when she revealed her sexuality to her parents, her mother asked God why he was cursing her. In the years we had been together up until that point, Jeana had also made multiple passive comments suggesting she was a "curse" or "cursed." If you listen close enough you will hear people's unconscious talking.

Judy looked at me, confused and then horrified as the memory of that day surfaced. Imagine a child hearing that they are a curse from God from the people who are supposed to love, nurture, and protect them. I asked Judy why she believed that because I was curious, knowing that she also had a gay brother, and I felt like there was more.

Judy's brother David died during the AIDS epidemic. He was her best friend. During this era, people linked gay, AIDS, and death. When Jeana came out, Judy's mind linked her daughter's revelation to her brother's death. In that moment, Judy felt cursed, not because her daughter was gay, but because she feared losing her just as she lost David. Jeana didn't hear this internal dialogue; she only heard the words spoken aloud. She heard part of her mom's story. And for decades, that is what her unconscious mind recorded as reality.

When I suggested that Judy share this revelation with Jeana, it was clear she needed time to comprehend what Jeana had believed all these years. About a month later, Jeana got an unexpected call from her mother. Judy explained her reaction all those years ago, revealing her fear and explaining her words. That night, Jeana told me about their brief conversation, and I asked how she felt about it. She was still processing it. In time, however, Judy's words offered Jeana's unconscious mind a chance to heal.

Only a couple of years after the conversation Jeana had with her mother, Judy suddenly passed away. I can't imagine how Jeana would have felt if they'd never had that talk. Judy's courage to revisit and share her true feelings gave Jeana a gift, the opportunity to heal a long-held, deep wound—a gift I am deeply grateful for.

Thank you, Judy.

Have you ever had an experience that shaped your perception of your worth? Maybe you've been in situations where you weren't wrong, but the other person's perspective was different because of their own experiences or age. Perhaps it's time to ask questions about something that still bothers you or to help someone else by sharing the whole story. By doing so, you can create a ripple effect of healing and growth, not just for yourself but for those around you. What could change in your life if you took that first step?

2ND COURSE

When I was a kid, I ate simple foods like cornflakes, canned green beans, pasta with tomato sauce, and Stouffer's® pizzas. I still remember the way the searing hot cheese from the boxed pizza would cling to the roof of my mouth with each bite, the extra crunchy crust tearing up my gums. Yet, every now and again I would try something that had layers and flavors like pepper steak. I had a complicated relationship with dishes like pepper steak because like many kids I did not want my foods to touch. I definitely didn't want to eat peppers in any form yet enjoyed the subtle flavor they gave to steak when sauteed in a pan together.

My mom would cook up a pan full of bright green and red bell peppers with thin slices of beef. It smelled fantastic but was denied by my picky palate. I'd strategically pick out the beef from the pan as it was cooking, isolating the peppers off to the side. I wasn't interested in the textures or depth of a dish. I wouldn't even eat those tiny onions on a McDonald's hamburger. I just wanted to enjoy my meal without interference from peppers that I felt were a violation of taste and texture.

Fast forward to my junior year in college when I moved into my first house. Knowing that I liked to create and experiment, I bought a classic Betty Crocker cookbook in paperback and decided I was going to learn how to cook more than mac 'n' cheese. I figured that if I could read, I could cook. Eventually, and with enough practice I started to get the hang of combining flavors and textures, occasionally experimenting with my own versions of recipes. It was then that I learned you cannot make a quiche with skim milk. My culinary evolution led me back to peppers, and I decided to give them another chance. To my surprise I liked them.

I still don't know if the younger me was stubborn and rooted in my dislike for peppers or if my palate changed. It's funny how we evolve, isn't it? Back then, I couldn't have imagined craving the very thing I used to discard, but that's how growth works. We change our minds, we see new perspectives. We develop a taste for things we once dismissed, whether it's in the kitchen or in life. Even when we evolve, other people sometimes still hold onto old perceptions of us. Take my mom, for example. Twenty years after I'd left Ohio, she moved to be closer to me. For at least two years, every time she came over for dinner she was shocked I was a good cook. It's like I was permanently stuck in her mind as that kid who picked out only the steak from the pepper steak pan, and the young adult still learning how to cook from a cookbook.

My growth didn't freeze when I left Ohio, but somehow, in her memory, it did. It's a reminder of how *we sometimes struggle to see people as they are now rather than who they used to be.* Our memories, and the way we hold on to them, shape us more than we care to admit. We become attached to a specific version of ourselves or others, and it can be hard to let go. We cling to comfort zones, to what's familiar, even when it stops serving us. But life, with all its unpredictability, has a way of nudging us forward, whether we're ready for it or not. It challenges our stubborn perspectives, asking us to look again and see things differently.

And that's not just about food. It's about giving people, including ourselves, the room to grow. We get so attached to certain images of who we think people are, just like my mom did with me and my cooking, that we miss out on seeing how far they've come. Sometimes, it's about learning to let others evolve, about acknowledging that even the things that once felt unnecessary or unwanted, like those peppers I used to shove aside, can end up being the very thing that completes the experience.

Growth isn't always about massive, life-altering moments; sometimes it's about subtle shifts. It's about noticing when we're holding onto outdated ideas or when we need to revisit something we've dismissed. It's about gaining new perspectives and embracing an empathetic approach to life—both towards us and others.

It's so easy to believe we understand someone based on a single encounter or a snapshot of their life, but people are multi-dimensional. Beneath what we see is a whole host of experiences, traumas, joys, and doubts. We carry baggage that's sometimes obvious and sometimes hidden, and all of it shapes how we act and react. Yet, how often do we give people the benefit of the doubt? How often do we stop and wonder, "What am I assuming? What am I missing here?"

It's a question I've learned to ask myself more and more, especially in my work. Most of us need to dig beneath our surface assumptions to uncover the real issues that are keeping us stuck—and it's rarely what we think it is. Most of the time, there's an outdated story running in a loop, an old narrative that needs a fresh perspective.

Growth is not a neat, linear process, it's messy. Sometimes it's painful, awkward, or downright uncomfortable, like trying a new dish you're convinced you won't like, only to find that it surprises you.

I've witnessed firsthand how transformative it is to shift your perspective, sometimes with a simple reframe. It can change a fleeting moment, a lifelong belief, or a relationship. We all make assumptions about each other, often without realizing it, and those assumptions can create barriers. Maybe it's a comment that hits us the wrong way or a person who annoys us because they don't fit our expectations. But what if we paused and asked ourselves, "Is there more to this?" What if we chose to be curious rather than judgmental?

The more I work with people, the more I see how much our experiences influence the stories we tell ourselves. We get hung up on judgments, the ones others impose on us and the ones we impose on ourselves. And sometimes, those judgments keep us from growing. They keep us from connecting. I've met people who hold onto their past mistakes, as if not letting go gives them some kind of control, and other people who let outdated views of themselves or others stop them from evolving. It's not easy to break free from those narratives, but it's so necessary.

Sometimes growth is about learning to let go of rigid expectations. It's about recognizing that balance doesn't mean control; it means being present and being aware. It's about knowing when to hold on and when to let go. Life invites us to keep tasting, to keep exploring, and to keep evolving. It's a process, one that asks us to approach people and situations with a spirit of curiosity, even when it's uncomfortable. Because when we do, we open ourselves up to a world of new possibilities.

Empathy, much like trying a new flavor, isn't something that happens passively. It was certainly not a gift given to me. It's a choice. It's deciding to see someone else's experience through their eyes, even when it's hard or doesn't make sense to us. It's about recognizing that everyone is doing the best they can with what they have. I've seen how powerful it can be when we stop trying to "fix" people or make generalized assumptions. Imagine all the doors you might have closed or possibilities you have ignored because of assumptions you've made. By leading with curiosity about other people and their perspectives we aren't just making space for them; we're also creating room for our own growth.

At the end of the day, we're all works in progress. We're constantly shifting and changing, even when it doesn't feel like it. *Our way isn't the only way, and our truth isn't the only truth.* The people we love, the ones who drive us crazy, and the strangers who irritate us all have backstories we can't see. We all bring our own baggage and our own hopes to the table. And when we approach each other with compassion and curiosity it makes for a more enjoyable experience. Life is full of flavors, and sometimes, the thing you thought you'd hate—like those bell peppers I used to avoid—turns out to be exactly what you needed all along.

Is There More?

I've been told I'm *such* a Virgo, which I take to mean I'm a planner, a doer, and someone who organizes chaos. I've always been a fixer, a helper, the kind of person who sees the whole recipe while everyone else is still chopping onions.

But eventually, you realize that being good at organizing the outside world doesn't mean you understand what the people in it actually need. You can get so caught up in doing things right, for yourself and everyone else, that you lose sight of the people themselves. You're so busy cooking that you don't realize no one is eating.

That realization didn't come quickly for me. I spent years solving problems, thinking everyone wanted to know my "better" way of doing something. Because why wouldn't you want to be more efficient? I wanted to know. But empathy isn't about showing someone the way. It's about giving them space to find their way, even if it's slower, messier, or looks nothing like your own.

I learned this through my own growth, especially during a breakup in my mid-thirties and the therapy I initially resisted. Once I committed, I was all in—devouring material like a hungry caterpillar. Reading about Imago theory made a profound impact. It's the idea that we unconsciously choose partners who mirror the wounds of our childhood, giving us a chance to heal and grow through relationships. That new lens shifted my perspective. I stopped being as reactive and defensive and started asking better questions—ones that considered other filters, not just mine.

It changed how I saw my clients, my friends, and especially how I communicated in my relationships. I began to understand that people don't just hear your words, they feel your words. Even something as simple as asking someone to pick up their socks might cause them to feel like a scolded child. And when that energy hits an old wound, it doesn't matter how "calm" or "matter of fact" you thought you were being.

Knowing this has made me a better person and partner. I saw this clearly one day with Jeana, not long after we bought our house. I came home before her and noticed she had left the back door unlocked.

"Hey," I said casually, "you left the back door unlocked."

She looked at me. "Okay."

But something was off, I could feel her energy shift.

"Did you *hear* what I said, or did what I said make you *feel* something?" I asked.

She shrugged. "Yeah, I know, I'm an idiot who can't even remember to lock a door."

I shook my head. "That's not what I said. That's what *you* told yourself. I'm not mad. You're not an idiot. And there will be times I leave the door unlocked, too."

"Sometimes a reminder is just a reminder. We'll both need them."

That moment stuck with me because the old me wouldn't have realized she didn't hear me as much as she *felt* an interpretation of what I said.

Understanding is about knowing facts and grasping the logic behind someone's situation. Empathy is about connecting emotionally to what they're feeling, even when you don't share the experience or fully understand the why. While I thought what I said to Jeana was just a reminder, I knew enough about her to realize there was more.

Meanwhile, in the years since, we have both reminded each other of little things—like leaving the indoor cat outside all day (oops!).

Empathy is knowing when to speak, when to listen, and when to shut up and let people have their own experiences. It's knowing the difference between feedback and judgment and understanding that even neutral words can carry weight depending on who's hearing them and what baggage they're carrying. It's about pausing and asking, *What's shaping their view? What don't I know yet?*

When a client says, "I've been eating clean," I ask, "What does clean mean to you?" If someone says, "I've been off track lately," I ask, "How long is lately?" Because without clarity, I'll give feedback based on *my* version of their reality.

We weren't all raised in the same kitchen. Even if we had access to the same ingredients: discipline, love, pressure, and expectations, we cooked different meals. And we keep doing it as adults. Your siblings may have grown up under the same roof, but they walked away with a completely different recipe.

Empathy isn't just about the hard stuff either. It shows up when someone says, "How can you like that band? They're terrible." Instead of defending your taste, you could ask, "What don't you like about them?" That tiny shift from defending to exploring can completely change the tone of the conversation.

It took a long time to recognize that my idea of what works isn't the only valid one. Other people's truths don't have to make sense to me or you. They just have to make sense to them. We don't need to agree with everyone. It's about understanding that most people, even the frustrating ones, are doing the best they can with what they've got. Sometimes they want a solution. Sometimes they just want to be seen or heard.

I still screw up, but my fuse is longer now. I'm more patient, less quick to correct, more open to being wrong, or just quiet. Growth isn't about getting the recipe perfect. It's learning to adjust the seasoning as you go.

We're all navigating life with our own map. And while our paths may cross, they don't have to match. We're all trying to get through the best we can—one reminder, one unlocked door at a time—each of us cooking with ingredients no one else got to see.

Eye Roll

"So disrespectful."

I overheard this muttered on a New York subway from an older couple standing near me. They glared at a teenage boy who was manspreading on the bench in front of us, completely absorbed in his phone. They had just boarded, and their irritation was obvious.

People think teens and toddlers are the masters of the eye roll, but honestly, elderly people are right there with them. It's a silent scolding—an eye roll or side eye, sometimes with a mutter for extra effect. I can't say I didn't agree with the couple. I was raised to think that not offering your seat to someone older was inconsiderate. But now, being in that space between generations, I get it. I can see both sides, especially with the decline of tight-knit communities and the captivating nature of technology.

That couple wasn't living in a world where technology pulls you in and makes everything else disappear. But for many of us, it's a reality. The teenager was probably not intentionally acting disrespectfully; he was just lost in his own world.

Without saying anything to the couple, I tapped the kid on the leg. He looked up, startled, as if I had just pulled him out of a dream. I motioned for him to take out an earbud and said, "Hey, maybe you could let that older couple sit and you can stand over here near me." He paused, blinked, then looked in the direction I motioned to see the couple. As if they suddenly appeared, he quickly stood up. The couple, still annoyed, sat down without a word. They didn't seem willing to accept that the kid wasn't even aware of his surroundings. Because frankly, the unawareness itself can be annoying and unsafe.

It's funny, isn't it? We make all these assumptions about people without knowing what's really going on. I stepped in because I knew the couple wasn't going to ask for the seat themselves, and it would've just made the ride uncomfortable for all of us. I knew I didn't feel like listening to grumbling on my ride. So, I figured, why not take the chance? It was a 50/50 shot—the kid could've blown me off.

Have you ever noticed how much better things go when we just ask for what we want? Sure, the answer could be "no," but you might be surprised by how willing people are to help when they're simply aware of the situation.

Towels

I had a breakup, the kind that untangles more than just your relationship. Seven years together, and most outsiders had no idea there were problems. The end didn't come all at once, and the unraveling showed up in strange ways. Like in cheap kitchen towels.

The Christmas before my ex and I broke up, she handed me a three-pack of holiday kitchen towels. No wrapping, no note. Just three towels—one red, one green, one white. Pretty sure she just grabbed them off the clearance rack at a drugstore that day. And they weren't even *good* towels. You know the kind: stiff, scratchy, and useless for anything other than pushing water around.

Then came her excuse. "I ran out of time."

I don't believe in "running out of time" unless there is a true miscalculation of time or effort required. Christmas doesn't sneak up on you. It's been coming for 365 days. When someone says they "ran out of time," what they're really saying is, "I didn't prioritize this." And if that's the truth, I'd rather you just own it. Say, "I forgot" or "I didn't plan properly, and I'm sorry." I can respect that. What I can't respect is pretending that lack of effort is about time, when it's clearly about care.

Jeana calls them "the towels heard 'round the world," referencing the opening shot of the Lexington and Concord battle. She's not wrong. That moment was a turning point. I still have two of the towels at work to clean up messes. Which, honestly, feels fitting.

The towels weren't the problem. Not really. They were just the most obvious symptom of something that had been unraveling for a while.

When you're in survival mode, whether in life or in a relationship, you stop showing up for each other. You get lazy. You focus on your own needs, and you forget what the other person values.

Gifts are my primary love language, not because I need *stuff* but because I value thoughtfulness. It was like she loaded my teenage self's dinner plate with gross peppers but no steak. A bag of peanut butter cups or gummy bears would've landed better because at least it would've shown she'd thought of my interests. It's not about what something costs, it's about what it says: "I see you. I know you. And I care." That's what was missing.

And that's how most things end, isn't it? The effort fades. The thoughtfulness disappears. And eventually, you're left holding a cheap towel and a clear understanding of where you stand.

Road Trips

While visiting my wife's sister, Amy, and her family, the topic of car shopping came up. Jeana had briefly left the room, and Amy and I began talking about their hunt for a vehicle with second-row captain's chairs. Curious, I asked why this feature was so important to her.

Amy explained that as a family of four, having individual seats for the kids was important. She went on to share a childhood memory of what road trips were like for her, the youngest of three.

Her older siblings would claim the window seats, leaving Amy in the center of the bench seat. While her siblings could use their respective windows as makeshift headrests, Amy did not have that luxury. Each time she would attempt to rest her head against the shoulder of either sibling she was promptly bumped off, leaving her head uncomfortably bobbing in the center for the entire journey.

Just as Amy finished recounting this story, Jeana returned to the room. I turned to her and joked, "Hey, I hear you were a real dick as a kid." With the innocence of no context she responded, "Why, what did I do?" Her shoulders shrugged; hands lifted in curiosity.

Without directly answering, I casually asked, "So what were road trips like for you as a kid." "They were great," Jeana replied cheerfully. Then I proceeded to summarize Amy's version, and we all giggled a little bit, albeit with a playful grumble from Amy.

Their very different viewpoints on road trips are a reminder that perspective is everything. One person may love the texture of cottage cheese while another gags at the thought of it. Sometimes we need to sit in someone else's "backseat" and see a situation through their window.

Bushes

"They are so inconsiderate."

I've thought that countless times while walking my dogs, dodging overgrown branches and bushes spilling onto the sidewalk as I pass a neighborhood house. Every walk becomes an obstacle course, pulling my dogs through the thorn and weed-infested tree lawn instead, trying to keep their paws safe from sand spurs and beggarweed.

David's backyard sits on the corner, enclosed by a chain-link fence, with bushes and tree branches that grow wild along the edge of his property and overtake the sidewalk. I don't know him beyond the occasional "hello" in passing. In fact, I walked by his house for years without ever seeing him or his dog. I don't even know if he lives alone or with others.

We only recently met during one of my walks when our dogs sniffed at each other through the fence. My terrier mix, Birdie, being her usual self, barked with her piercing tone until she decided she was finished. Though Jeana and I consider ourselves the masters of our dogs, we admittedly lack control in a few key areas, one being excessive barking at other animals.

Before ever talking to him, I decided that David's household didn't care about its overgrown landscaping's impact on passersby. I resigned myself to the fact that nothing would change and stopped giving it much thought years ago. Then one day I realized—maybe they don't even know. From inside the yard, it probably just looks like a tree and some bushes growing into their yard's space. How often do they walk on the side of the house where the bushes are spilling over? I'm hyper-aware of things like that because of all those years of apartment living—sharing walls, ceilings, and floors. You do your best to be courteous and accept the reality of shared walls. Not everyone has that same perspective.

So, I made a decision: the next time I saw David I would ask if he would trim back the overgrown landscaping. A few weeks later I had my chance. I explained the situation and David said he hadn't even noticed the sidewalk since they don't walk the elderly dog. He told me he would cut them down that day, and he did. It's easy to assume someone is inconsiderate, but sometimes things just go unnoticed or simply aren't valued the way you value them.

Echo Chambers

We're living in a time where the definitions of *exposure* and *indoctrination* have become incredibly conflated. It's as if we've forgotten that being exposed to new ideas or different beliefs doesn't mean we're being told to accept them. It means we're learning, observing, and experiencing something outside our norm. It's like sitting at a table where the group orders a bunch of appetizers—you're not obligated to taste every one, but you're aware they exist and that others enjoy them. Yet somehow, we've reached a point where simply seeing or hearing something unfamiliar is treated like a threat. That confusion has fed a culture of polarization and isolation where difference isn't just misunderstood, it's feared.

For example, the way television stations capture a specific market and cater their news to that group. It's almost like living in an echo chamber, where you're constantly fed the same ideas, perspectives, and opinions you already hold. I'm wise enough to know that when I went dress shopping for a wedding, I only needed to put a little bit of effort into searching the web for options before I was bombarded with ad targeting from retailers. Much like ad targeting, the same holds true for the social media platforms themselves, the algorithm feeds you more and more of what you seek. While that can be okay, the questions I like to raise are, "How often do you seek out a differing perspective?" and "Do you research multiple perspectives to determine if something is closer to the truth or a lie?"

The media, and now real life, are leaving little room for alternative thoughts. It's like a verse from *Good Help* by Death Cab for Cutie which basically says that you never hear "no" when your friends are on the payroll. And really, isn't that what we're seeing today? Is that really what you want? If we're only listening to clones of ourselves, that's all we'll know. We won't become more understanding, worldly, cultured, empathetic, or even open with ourselves. When we see only one side of things, we tend to believe that's the only side that exists. In truth, and keeping with quoting musicians and payrolls as inspiration, "a real friend or mentor is not on your payroll." Well-stated by Prince during his 2004 Rock & Roll Hall of Fame induction ceremony speech.

Exposure, at its core, should be about presenting information neutrally, encouraging dialogue, and allowing room for critical thinking at any age. It's about giving people the freedom to form their own opinions and learn about facts that might be uncomfortable.

Indoctrination, on the other hand, presents information in a way that pressures people to accept a particular belief or viewpoint, and discourages questioning and alternative perspectives.

The tricky part is that this boundary can become blurred, especially when repetition is involved. Think about it: if we're repeatedly exposed to a specific set of beliefs without hearing other perspectives, it doesn't matter how neutral that exposure was at the start. Over time, it can start to feel like indoctrination because we're not getting the full picture. This can happen in schools, workplaces, or even in everyday conversations, where authority figures like teachers, media personalities, family members, or religion influence our views. If someone in a position of power presents their personal beliefs as the only valid way to think, even unintentionally, that exposure can slide into indoctrination if you are not willing to be a critical thinker and seek out other sources, too.

Let's look at how history is taught. If a class only presents the narrative of the victors and conquerors, students miss out on the full story. It's not that teaching history is indoctrination, but by omitting alternative perspectives or minimizing them, it becomes a one-sided narrative. That's where the problem starts. What happens when we only hear one story and think it's the whole truth? Or we streamline an experience so concisely that we lose the complexities of any situation.

When you stop to see that most of life is multidimensional it enriches perspective. When we stop questioning, and we stop thinking critically it's a dangerous place to be and it stunts growth, both personal and societal.

But let's be real, some people are so deeply rooted in their beliefs that they see any exposure to alternative viewpoints as a threat. It's a fear-fueled reaction rooted in the belief that simply hearing something different will undermine everything they hold close. And, I get it, it is human nature to push back against something that feels challenging to our existence, whether physical or values-based.

There's a difference between exploring different ideas and being forced to accept them. I'm a firm believer in owning who you are and being okay with that. Just because someone else has a different value or belief doesn't mean yours is negated. Their belief isn't taking away from you, just like you being exposed to another way of thinking isn't threatening your core values. In fact, it's what helps you cement them even further if they really matter to you.

Take Critical Race Theory (CRT), for example. It's stirred up a lot of emotions, but at its core, it's about understanding how race has shaped our country's history. Is it really indoctrination to teach that white men held more power and opportunity in early America? Or is it just acknowledging how things were so we can better understand how things are?

But does that mean we need to make today's kids feel guilty or force them to apologize for something they didn't do? Absolutely not. Kids can still be kids.

At the heart of all this is how we handle exposure. Some people hear the word "gender" or "race" and immediately think someone's trying to brainwash their child. But hearing about something isn't the same as being told what to think about it. Exposure is not indoctrination.

A little girl who isn't into makeup or boys isn't automatically gay or trans. A boy who prefers art to football isn't confused about who he is.

It's okay to let kids explore without rushing to label them, or worse, forcing them into some narrow idea of what's "normal."

What's actually harmful is keeping kids and adults from learning about the world. We don't become grounded in who we are by being sheltered. We become grounded by being exposed to different perspectives, learning to think critically, and figuring out for ourselves what resonates with us.

We aren't safe because we've lived in a box. We're safe because we've learned how to navigate what's outside of it.

I've always been grateful for the diverse experiences and people I've encountered. These experiences didn't force me to change who I am; rather, they helped me relate to people who are different from me. They've also allowed me to discover parts of myself I didn't know existed but have been thrilled to discover. And if that's what people are afraid of—discovering something new about themselves or their beliefs—it gets labeled as indoctrination. But I find that ironic because the people who are crying indoctrination the loudest are often the same ones trying to force their beliefs on others.

We see this in political extremes, too. It's almost as if those extremes are more interested in pushing their own agenda than allowing for open, honest exposure. What they're really doing is indoctrinating others into their way of thinking, while accusing the other side of doing the same. Meanwhile, people like me, who tend to fall somewhere in the middle, are just sitting here thinking:

"Can't we allow both sides to exist without disparaging each other?"

"Can't we have educated conversations about tough topics without assuming that just hearing the other side is going to corrupt us?"

Respectable conversations where both parties don't necessarily agree are wonderful to hear.

One of the coolest things I got to do as a teenager, something taboo in most public schools today, was going on a field trip to multiple places of worship. This was part of my gifted education program, and with parental approval, we got to visit different spiritual centers and meet with religious leaders who explained their religion's beliefs, origins, and traditions. It was such a unique opportunity. I got to learn about people who were completely unlike me, and it didn't mean I was going to adopt their beliefs or practices. It simply gave me exposure to different ideas, and it allowed me to better understand the world around me. My religious choices today are based on my own understanding and evolution as a person, not because I was told what to believe.

Ultimately, we must ask ourselves: Are we so afraid of exposure that we're willing to live in an echo chamber where the only voices we hear are our own? Burying our heads doesn't make anything go away, but it does make people ill-prepared to deal with it when confronted. Are we so scared of the world that we refuse to engage with it unless it mirrors us? Life is spicy, and tasting it enriches the palate.

Consider this: if you don't know why you have a certain value or belief for something, can't state facts and reasons for following a political candidate or party, or you do something as an adult just because your family always did it that way—then you've been indoctrinated. Exposure to different ideas is not about losing ourselves; it's about gaining a deeper understanding of who we are and where we stand in relation to others.

Grandfather Clocks

Next to the front door of my grandparents' home stood a giant grandfather clock. It rarely worked because it was seldom wound. It had a glass front panel adorned with gold-colored designs around the edges, the clear glass ensured the golden pendulum and chimes were visible. The clock's face, though hazy in my memory, was ornate with silver and gold tones. Nearby, a handcrafted cartoonish wooden cuckoo clock was mounted on the wall. It occasionally signaled the time with its sharp 'cuckoo' as a tiny bird emerged from a small door.

When they both worked, I watched the grandfather clock's pendulum in a trance, waiting for the chimes to signal the hour while the cuckoo clock notified me at a slightly different time. These clocks were never in sync. Both required constant attention, and I often wound and over-wound them with their special keys, unaware of the delicate nature of their mechanisms. My interest in the clocks waxed and waned, likely influenced by my boredom, as I was always looking for something to observe or tinker with. Eventually, like many items in homes, they became silent relics of their era.

Years later, I thought of those clocks when my client Patricia, (referred to in my previous book, *Feeling Stuck?*), told me about hers. About six months after her husband passed away, Patricia had a crushing realization: she didn't know her financial situation, nor how to manage routine household tasks. Patricia was a dutiful wife in the style of the 1950s. Her life's focus was on her husband and children. She left her father's home and moved directly into her husband's, never feeling like she needed to learn certain things. We often talked about the life she wished she had beyond being a wife and mother, a version of herself she barely allowed space to imagine.

One day, she told me she needed her irrigation timer adjusted but didn't know how. Frustrated, she was mad at herself and her late husband. "Patricia, you don't know how to adjust the irrigation timer because you never had to, not because you can't learn how," I told her. I scribbled down some simple instructions and sent her off with a little note of encouragement.

The following week, Patricia came bounding in with the kind of excitement you'd see in a proud kid. "I did it! I changed the timer, and it worked!" she proclaimed, her face glowing. I celebrated her small victory, knowing just how big it really was for her. Then, with a little grin, she added, "And I also set the grandfather clock."

She explained how they'd had that clock for decades and that her husband always wound it. Since his death, it had become an object, no longer a functioning time piece. I was curious. "So how did you do it?" I asked. Patricia smiled. "Well, honey, you've shown me how you look stuff up on YouTube, so I thought I'd try it, too. I found a man who showed how to do it, and I found the key to wind it on the top in the same place he kept his." It turned out to be the same spot where my grandparents kept theirs, too.

Patricia's husband's death, while heartbreaking, had also removed a lid she didn't even know existed. For the first time, she had the space, and maybe the reason, to prove to herself just how capable she really was. That clock, once silent and neglected like so many things we take for granted, was ticking again because Patricia dared to try.

Both clocks, hers and mine, were beautiful, intricate, and demanding of attention. And like them, we can go silent when we're left unattended, or when we tell ourselves we can't do something just because we haven't done it before. Patricia reminded me that confidence is something we can build at any age. Sometimes it starts with a YouTube video. Sometimes it starts with a simple note from someone who believes in us. Either way, all it takes is the courage and willingness to try something new from the menu.

Repent! (Just Kidding)

"Hey girl, happy birthday. Call me later." My friend Aidi's bright and familiar voice on my answering machine. A lovely way to wake up. It was the morning of September 11, 2001.

A few minutes later, the answering machine called out another message, this time my mom's voice, void of any sense of timing or phone etiquette. "Hi Coley," she said, "Happy birthday. I can't believe there is so much terrorism on your birthday. Please call me back." At least she said "please," right?

Confused and a bit alarmed, I fumbled for the remote and turned on the television. Every channel filled the screen with horrifying images and messages.

Weeks passed in a blur of rising oil prices, surging nationalism, and a disturbing increase in attacks on Muslims. Not everyone had mobile phones yet, but dial-up internet made email communication very accessible.

Of my little pod of college best friends, most came from small towns with limited, narrow perspectives on life outside their communities. If bigoted and progressive were a scale, many of them leaned towards bigoted with college broadening their horizons a bit. Michelle leaned closest to the bigoted end of the spectrum. It had been a handful of years since graduation and she had moved to a much bigger city, one that had broadened her view of new people and experiences. Her tastes shifted far beyond the familiar comforts we all once clung to. What we didn't know was that she had shed her former views, evolving into a more open-minded and compassionate person.

In the weeks after 9/11, twenty-plus years ago, Michelle sent an email blast to a fairly long list of people. In it, she expressed her horror and outrage at the rising attacks on Muslims and the vandalism of their homes and businesses, sharing personal stories about her friends. She reminded us that no one's race or religion defines who they are, or makes them responsible for someone else's actions. She asked us to be mindful and look out for one another.

I remember this so profoundly because we get caught up in memories and expectations of who people were, either created by time and distance, or the longing for what we want to hold onto. Jobs and cities changed, and we all evolved, Michelle's email being a bold testament to her evolution. Though we might have expected her to remain neutral or indifferent, there she was, firmly stating her new beliefs and values. And we accepted them, allowing her to move forward as a new version of herself.

Repentance plays an important role in Judaism, Islam, and Christianity, and it's just as central in modern society. We expect people to own their mistakes, to grow, and to feel genuine regret. Yet even when they do, they often face ongoing scrutiny and punishment. If people want to judge Michelle for her past racist beliefs, they also need to recognize that her 2001 email wasn't just words, it was an act of repentance. A visible step showing who she was becoming.

Too often, people are repeatedly judged for their past, even if their former self was in step with the moral or cultural code at that time. The past molds us into our present self even if we no longer approve of our behavior from years ago. To move forward it is important to give yourself grace for being young, foolish, and making questionable choices. It acknowledges that your values may have dramatically shifted, and that's okay. It was a different version of you. You are the sum of your experiences, and they have led you to who you are now.

Loud

Why do we let the loudest, most extreme voices define the narrative when they rarely represent most people? Whether it's people of color, LGBTQ+, non-Christians, or women in male-dominated industries, the individuals I know are simply living their lives, working hard, loving their families, and contributing to society, just like everyone else. They're not the ones dominating the conversation. It's the ones demanding attention, often in the most provocative ways, that grab the spotlight.

We tend to lump people into groups, labeling them based on their race, gender, religion, or sexual orientation, without acknowledging their individuality, leaning on what we've heard from the loudest voices instead of seeing people for who they are. Maybe we can do a better job of seeing others, and ourselves, as multidimensional rather than the category they've been placed into.

Extreme ideologies can be suppressive, misaligned, or completely overshadow the values of the majority they supposedly represent. For example, I see too many stats about young Black men being racially aligned with criminal or violent behavior (even when they've shown no sign of it) simply because of their appearance. Criminals don't represent most of this population. Yet too often, these young men are told by their own communities and the world around them that the system is rigged against them before they've even had a chance to prove themselves. It almost encourages an "every man for himself" attitude.

While challenges absolutely exist, are we helping by stoking fear and anger, by telling these young men they must approach life with a chip on their shoulder and a take-all attitude? How can we expect someone to show up fully when they've been taught that opportunity has ended before it even started?

That's a limiting mindset.

Awareness is essential, but we don't have to reinforce the idea that life is set up to beat them down, or anyone, for that matter. Instead, let's focus on breaking the limiting beliefs that form early, the ones that say, "I'm less than," or "I'll never be enough."

Those beliefs aren't unique to any one group. In fact, they are the leading limiting beliefs I help my clients release no matter their sex, race, or religion.

Just like individuals carry limiting beliefs that were never theirs to begin with, entire communities get misrepresented by the loudest, most extreme voices speaking on their behalf. And once those voices dominate the spotlight, they begin shaping narratives, policies, and assumptions that don't reflect the true diversity within the group. It's like sitting at a table where a few people order for everyone while the rest quietly go along, even if the plate in front of them doesn't represent their taste or interest.

Of all the forms of Christianity, for example, somehow the most controlling, adversarial views get woven into government despite our alleged separation of church and state. I often wonder: where's the conversation about other faiths? Is there no room for their values? Are we unintentionally signaling to people of other religions that their beliefs don't matter as much? Or are they simply choosing to allow for individuality, rather than shouting their most divisive values in the face of everyone else?

In the LGBTQ+ community, I often wonder why the most extreme or flamboyant elements are the ones pushed to the forefront. It is okay for any collective to have its more fringe representations because that is part of individuality. But if you look at the average experience, most people are just living their lives with their own values, much like anyone else.

The media love to spotlight the loudest or most sensational aspects of a group, but the reality for most individuals within these communities is far more nuanced and more integrated into broader society.

I see a similar issue among women in the workplace, especially in industries where women are still in the minority. Too often, we step on each other to get ahead, as though there's only room for one of us at the top. The need to make a name for yourself trumping all else. Wouldn't it be better to lift each other up rather than tear each other down?

I had a female client who ran a commercial real estate business, a field dominated by men. Anna soon realized that in her industry, some women treated other women as disposable tools for advancement, or felt they had to play the "bitch card" to gain respect—moves that often backfired.

But Anna had a different mindset. She believed there was more than enough room for women to succeed in construction and real estate, and she made it a point to mentor other women without razing everyone she met. Her company flourished—not just because she worked hard, but because she understood the value of collaboration.

At the end of the day, it's about being confident in who you are and learning to integrate into society. *The loudest voices aren't always the most constructive, they're often the voices of conflict.*

Real change comes from everyday people quietly building bridges, connecting with those around them, and contributing to society in meaningful ways. What if we focused less on shouting and more on weaving the textures and flavors of society together? It's time we stopped letting the extremes define us and started remembering that most of us are already working, building, and living side by side.

Cards We Hide Behind

My mother grew up in a household that did its best with limited emotional intelligence. My grandparents, both hardworking and loving in their own ways, raised their children with the values they knew. My Old-World Italian grandmother was a cook, a beautician, and worked in a machine shop during World War II. She was a woman of many talents but also one of many harsh words. My grandfather, though loving, wielded the wooden spoon, one I met plenty as a child because I was a bit of a Gremlin.

From a young age, my mother soaked up the criticisms and judgments around her. "You have big calves," my grandma would say. Maybe it was just an observation. Maybe a comparison. Either way, it stuck—my mom referred to that comment many times as I grew up.

Even though my mother was a math whiz, the kids at school teased her because she was short and had trouble reaching the top of the blackboard when she went up to solve problems. And although she loved math, she didn't become a teacher like she wanted. Those words etched her psyche and shaped her self-image. Her insecurity about her height held her back.

Though intellectually confident and gregarious at times, her low self-esteem has been a constant undercurrent in her life. To this day, she frequently mentions her height: "Is my drink smaller because I am short?" "Did you sit there because I'm short." "You're probably wondering why I'm so short." She is, of course, bothered when someone comments on her height, too. Once just over five feet tall, age and scoliosis have taken six or so inches from her. Ironically, despite her offense at having height mentioned, she takes every liberty to ask unusually tall people how tall they are, believing they must not have any insecurities.

Growing up, I heard a myriad of excuses and "poor me" victim statements from my family. These were not just idle complaints but deeply ingrained beliefs that shaped their actions and decisions. As an observer it made me wonder if our lives were constantly under personal attack or perhaps some things just *are what they are.*

Eventually, I realized that sometimes we need to ask ourselves: *what cards are we hiding behind that limit our possibilities?* These cards, born out of unconscious fears of success or victim mindsets, serve as convenient excuses that cloud our vision and stunt our growth. They may hold some merit but are not the absolutes of life.

Admittedly, I get tired of people holding up these cards and acting as victims, as though these reasons are the only barriers holding them back. Too often, they project their learned judgments onto others unfairly. You can use the race card, the gender card, or any other card as an example and decide that is why you're not getting a promotion or why someone is looking at you a certain way. But you have to ask yourself: why are you using that card? Where did you get it from? And is it even real? Do you really not like vegetables? Or is it something you've told yourself since you were a kid forced to eat broccoli?

Sometimes these cards we hold are perceptions we have created, while others have been assigned. It's the young woman who is told that she needs to find a partner to take care of her, solidifying her belief that she is not competent on her own as a female. Or the young Black man, told by his family that the world will look down on him and to focus on taking what he wants, a mindset granting him mistrust and disconnection, and preventing him from opening his heart. Both are personal examples from people I've known during my adulthood.

Imagine for a moment that these cards don't exist. What would you attempt if you knew you couldn't fail? How would you act if you were free from the fear of judgment? The truth is, these cards are self-imposed limitations, often rooted in past experiences and societal expectations. But, they don't define your future. If they did, we would have no stories of people who truly achieved something remarkable yet unlikely.

I often look back at my family and the stories they told themselves. My grandparents, doing what they could with what they knew, didn't provide the emotional cuddles their children needed. This absence of nurturing left a void. My mother, her brother, and her sister knew they were loved, but each grew up navigating their experience in their unique ways. My mother, despite her many strengths, often let her insecurities and perceived shortcomings dictate her behaviors, fueling what I later learned was anxiety attachment. This attachment style creates an unconscious fear of being unloved, often showing up as jealousy and other fear-based characteristics.

Can you imagine how much internal strife she has endured? How much easier could life have been up until now if she had not spent so much time seeking external validation, knowing that she was enough just as she was?

Have you ever not applied for a job or promotion because you decided you were too old, undeserving, or unready? Is that even real? If you did hold yourself back, ask yourself why. Are you hiding behind a card that prevents you from trying, from risking failure, and ultimately from succeeding?

Sometimes we crave success but unconsciously fear it, perhaps realizing we don't know what to do if we achieve it, or fearing we can't sustain it. Or, that someone might label us as frauds. And how many truly believe that the card they hold up is the actual reason they're held back, rather than the card itself inhibiting their growth? I have been in this position and it's frustrating, and I'm grateful that I used my own coaching tools to get out of my own way.

There's an excellent scene in an episode of the drama series, *This Is Us*, where the character Kate, an overweight woman who used to sing, decides to audition as a singer again. She gets on stage, sings briefly, and is dismissed with a "thank you, next." After the audition, she tells the club manager it was unfair, suggesting her weight was the issue and stating that she was not going to let him judge her based on her appearance. He says nothing, then asks another woman, who is already on the stage, to sing. She's excellent. The manager tells Kate that weight wasn't the problem; she needed practice and had several areas to work on, all of which Kate agreed with.

Without that discussion, because Kate held onto her weight as the obstacle preventing her from getting what she wanted, she would not have been able to see the real problem and identify a path for growth. I discuss this scene in a workshop I host about overcoming obstacles and limiting beliefs because I believe it is a powerful metaphor for how we often blind ourselves with the cards we hide behind.

If you think about your own cards, what obstacles keep you from learning and growing? What cards are you hiding behind that you use as an excuse for not reaching your potential? Are you too old, too young, too short, too tall, too fat, too thin, inexperienced, or overqualified, or are you defined by your skin tone or sex? Are these real barriers, or are they just excuses?

Imagine what you could achieve if you decided that those cards don't define you. The path to growth starts with the realization that we are often our biggest obstacle. It's time to rewrite your story. I sign all of my books with a single phrase, "This Is Your Time." It's time to embrace the possibilities that have always been there for you.

Pick Up the Phone!

Please, please, stop waiting for other people to initiate your life. Pick up the phone. Call someone, send a text, an email, or a carrier pigeon if that's what it takes. Make a genuine effort to connect with people, understanding that they, like you, might be busy. And yes, be prepared to follow up.

I've lost count of how many times I've heard someone complain about not hearing from a friend or loved one. Our conversation often follows a path like this:

Stephanie: I haven't heard from Amy in a long time. Do you hear from her?

Me: No.

Steph: I wonder why she hasn't called.

Me: Are you interested in talking to her?

Steph: Sure, but I guess she is busy / I did something...

Me: Have you called or sent a text?

Steph: No.

Me: Why not? If you want to talk to her or find out how she is then ask her.

Steph: She can call me, too. / I don't want to bother her.

Me: And you can call her, too. Why are you waiting to hear from someone? She might be thinking the same about you. If you want to hear from Amy, reach out.

Too often, people get caught up in waiting for others to take the first step in their relationships instead of being proactive and creating the connections they desire. If you want to see a movie with someone, ask them. There are only three possible outcomes: they say "yes," "no," or propose an alternative time or plan.

If the answer is "no" try someone else. And if you can't find another companion, I challenge you to go alone. As kids, getting caught going to the theater alone felt like social suicide, but as adults, it's about taking charge and giving yourself the freedom to do what you enjoy, whether or not you have company.

Opportunities and enjoyment will pass you by if you spend your life waiting for others to reach out or initiate experiences. By taking the first step, we empower ourselves to build the relationships and experiences we want, fostering independence and resilience, and giving others the passive "permission" they need to become more proactive in their life, too. So, try dining alone and order the scallop carpaccio. Even if it feels uncomfortable, you might find that you like both.

Belonging

The yearning for belonging will not end because humans are social creatures. In fact, *The Handbook of Experimental Existential Psychology* explains that belonging is necessary for overall development and well-being.

Before technology, you were literally physically seen or unseen. You were invited to a party, or you weren't. People saw you at the Friday night football game or they didn't. There was no live streaming or socializing alone in your bedroom via some social app. We had to call friends, talk to their parents, and go to each other's houses to hang out. Plus, most of us had a job at 16 years old, if not before because we were babysitting or doing some other casual means of employment. These things helped develop our sense of belonging.

As a coach, I've had a wonderful opportunity to work with people ages 8 to 98. Some of the most rewarding experiences I've had come from working with teens. How kids experience the world is much different than mine at that age, of course. Isn't that true of every generation? Years ago, I was working with a young lady in fitness and wellness. We met for two hours each week. Over time, she shared bits and pieces about her life and her feelings. She explained that while she had friends, she didn't feel like she could really connect with them because it often felt like people were putting on a show for social media likes. Furthermore, she did not feel like she had a specific group she belonged to. She was not an athlete, or in choir, drama club, or any other school organization, and didn't have a specific pod she wanted to run with all the time.

As a high schooler, she wasn't certain who her group was, instead having individual friends rather than a consistent friend collective. In her words, she felt like "a side piece," regularly bouncing around different groups because she liked different things about each group or person.

I looked at her with empathy for her experience, reflected back to her what she felt, then I asked, "Have you ever considered that you don't belong anywhere, because you belong everywhere?"

She looked at me in the way that I felt when I realized the same for myself many years ago: free. Free to accept the ability to connect with many people. Sometimes a simple reframe of perspective is what is needed to move forward.

Voice

I was at the Boys and Girls Club one afternoon, talking to a group of kids about the power of using your voice. I told them that no matter what anyone has told you to believe, your voice matters. Every single one of us has something worth sharing, and learning to speak up in a way that's honest but not rude or cruel is a skill that can change so much in your life. For kids, as a subordinate member of a home, it sometimes seems like their thoughts and opinions are not valued. And for some, it is what they are taught—a lesson that can transcend adulthood.

We learn by being curious, grow by pushing ourselves out of our comfort zones, and inspire others by showing up in a way that makes a difference. That's why one of my mottos is: *Learn. Grow. Inspire.*®

That afternoon, I wanted those kids to know that their words have value and that they should never let anyone make them feel small or unimportant. Even if the world sometimes makes them feel like their voice doesn't count, they have something worth sharing.

Speaking up doesn't just help you, it gives others permission to do the same. When I practiced martial arts, I often asked questions while learning new forms or techniques, even when I already knew the answers. Not because I needed them, but because I knew others did, a habit I learned from Jonathan who was higher ranked than me.

Some people stay silent because they're embarrassed. Others don't even know enough yet to ask. Either way, when one person speaks, it breaks the ice. It signals that it's safe to not know everything, and safe to learn out loud. Using your voice isn't just about getting what you need; it's about making it easier for others to find theirs, too.

My friend Holly, who I met through karate, once told me how much she appreciated that I asked questions. She knew I wasn't asking for myself, but to fill the gaps for people. Holly took that idea and now applies it to her work life. In meetings, she'll ask relevant questions to fill the voids she knows exist for some of her colleagues. It's a simple act, but has a huge impact—providing clarity and understanding for her team.

I shared this story with the kids, hoping they'd see how small, thoughtful actions can inspire others, and give them the power to learn and speak up for what they need. I reminded them that you never know who you might help when you choose to use your voice. There's so much value in learning how to communicate clearly and respectfully. It's not about being loud or dominating a conversation; it's about sharing in a way that validates your needs and makes space for others, too.

When working with organizational teams, I remind them that communication isn't just about driving home your point; it's about doing so in a way that is relevant to their group to foster understanding and collaboration. Whether it's in a meeting at work, in a conversation with your partner, or even with your kids, the way you deliver your message matters. We've all seen how harsh words or a defensive tone can shut people down, but when you speak with intention and respect, you create a positive environment.

Whether you're asking a question in class, sharing your feelings with a friend, or contributing to a work meeting, your words have the potential to make an impact. Speaking up is not just helping you learn and grow, you're also paving the way for others to feel safe and encouraged to share their voices, too.

Identity

It's striking how many people latch onto a single facet of their identity and make it their defining feature. "I am female." "I am gay." "I am Black." "I am Jewish." "I am Christian." They turn adjectives into nouns and sometimes allow that single trait to eclipse the entirety of their being, almost as if it's the only aspect of their identity worth noticing. It's like they're constantly broadcasting, "I'm (noun) and proud!" which, while being a positive assertion, can sometimes overshadow their individuality, and clump them into the toxic qualities of the fringe.

For more than three decades, I've navigated the complex landscape of intimate relationships with both women and men. In the earlier days, my sexual fluidity had more to do with alcohol and curiosity than anything else, and over time I found myself developing romantic relationships based more on connection rather than genitals. As I sit here today, one might identify me as a gay person because I have a wife. And while that makes sense, my best of friends seem to have embraced the concept that I am simply a person who does, in fact, have a wife.

Admittedly, as a younger person, I pushed back at the gay label more, associating it with the extreme; the groups of people whose central identity is their gayness, and who insisted that others must deal with it by dousing you with it like a fire hose. I remember being a straight college student with a single gay female friend, whose other gay friends felt they needed to do their best to make social situations with me uncomfortable with their language or their actions. "Look, fresh meat." "Did you bring us a new one to convert?"

My friend told her friends to back off because they were being predatory in the way youth and alcohol mix at any bar. Or watching extreme displays of debauchery and sexual overtures played through like theater on the College Green, a common place for students to read, play frisbee or just relax. The participants insisted that any discomfort we felt was because of our bigoted views of their gayness. By pushing their identity so forcefully, it seemed less about celebrating it but rather, perhaps unknowingly, pushing people away. In hindsight, perhaps it represented the way many of them had felt alienated.

In general, College Green was the place where anyone wanting to be in the spotlight could light up the central part of campus with their sometimes-aggressive messaging like insisting people were sinners and going to Hell, or really any group looking for reasons to argue.

Then, much like now, I am fairly centrist in my beliefs and thinking, which has made extremes of any group off-putting to me because they often seem to be an inaccurate or fringe representation of the group they represent. Their voices are simply the loudest. Rarely do you hear chill, happy, centrist people of any group making a lot of commotion; perhaps that is the problem.

Can you imagine living like that, seeing yourself as only one part of a whole, and missing out on the wholeness of your full identity? It can be as simple as me asking my client Joe, who was unfulfilled in his quest to find intellectually similar friends, if he had considered seeking straight friends, too. He looked at me puzzled. Though not closed to the idea, he told me he had not considered it because in his mind he was gay, and as a result, all his needs would need to come from the gay community. This perspective always fascinated me because, unlike many, I never saw myself as just one thing. I am a web of qualities, interests, and characteristics, each contributing to the person I am today. So are you.

While out with a friend's teenage daughter a few years ago and amid a complex discussion about gender identity, she told me she didn't want to be seen as only female descriptors, and then proceeded to insert gender words to describe herself. I reminded her that she is more than feminine or masculine and asked her to describe herself without using words like "boyish," "girlie," "masculine," "feminine," and so on. She struggled. In fact, even with probing from me, she could not wrap her head around my request. Then I described myself. I told her I was a person, I was active, curious, and interested in people. I have a wife, pets, and enjoy good discussions, and so on. She looked at me and said, "Hmm, I'm gonna have to think about that." I smiled then we returned to our previous discussion about skateboarding.

Over the years it has occurred to me that the need to explicitly state and identify who you are comes from various places:

- Perhaps the need to make yourself comfortable with a new belief about yourself, such as accepting that you no longer want to follow your family's religion or becoming comfortable in your sexuality (you reject that part of self because you have consciously moved from it);
- Denying something your higher self believes you are, but you cannot consciously accept (consider the many occasions we've heard about people who have assaulted gays as actually being closeted themselves); or,
- Something as basic as trying on new "skin" and convincing yourself to be comfortable with this new experience.

Have you ever noticed how some people fight relentlessly to be heard, to have a particular part of their identity or values acknowledged by the extreme of the opposite side of the spectrum rather than meeting people closer to the center? So accustomed to fighting for a single element of their identity, they forget about their wholeness or mutability. Consider politics, if we were able to isolate sections, the extreme right and left tend to fight it out, while the middle cluster tends to work it out.

Imagine now, two opposing sides of the spectrum looking to have their identity survive. We see it in political and religious extremes often. Rather than believing there can be a co-existence among values, the extremes of the spectrum sometimes force their whole belief system onto the other side as if co-existence is a Zero-Sum Game, leaving one side to win while the other loses.

Are there aspects of your identity that you push to the forefront, perhaps to the point of overshadowing the rest of who you are? Maybe it's your skin tone, your sexuality, your religion, or another characteristic. Do you feel that if you don't emphasize this part of you, it might go unnoticed, or unvalidated? Imagine what it would feel like to simply be content in your skin, to embrace all facets of your identity without feeling the need to highlight one over the others.

I've found peace in being content with the entirety of who I am. My various identities are not fragmented pieces fighting for recognition but rather, they coexist harmoniously within me. I no longer need to prove or validate any single part of myself to others.

Next time you find yourself leaning heavily into one part of your identity, ask yourself: Why? Are you seeking validation, acceptance, or perhaps understanding? And what might happen if you let go of that need and embraced the full spectrum of who you are? Would you feel more balanced, more at peace? Would your relationships become more genuine and fulfilling? Imagine the profound impact this shift in perspective could have on your life?

There's a certain freedom in this acceptance. It allows you to move through life with a sense of ease, interacting with people and forming connections based on the totality of who you are. You're not just a label or a category; you're a complex, multifaceted individual with unique experiences, interests, and traits, just like a fine dining tasting menu.

3RD COURSE

Jeana once told me she loved that I'm always looking to grow. At first, I took it as a huge compliment because I genuinely believe our purpose is to keep evolving. But as it turns out, she was just happy that I was willing to learn how to snowboard, even as I teetered on the cusp of my forties. Here I thought I was being recognized for some admirable quality, but really it was about my willingness to strap my feet to a board with hopes I didn't spend the day tumbling backward downhill; something I did a lot when I started.

It's interesting how our appetites change as we age—not just in the literal sense, but in the way we approach risks, set boundaries, and redefine what we'll tolerate. With snowboarding I approached its challenges, and risk-reward ratio differently than I might have in my twenties. With age comes experiences and new wisdom. You weigh your options more carefully, like deciding whether to indulge in a rich dessert or stick to something lighter. But risk isn't just about avoiding broken bones; it's also about breaking old patterns, pushing past outdated perceptions, and becoming someone who aligns with your current values. And the best part? You can choose to start adjusting those "portions" of your life anytime.

When we're younger, we hand out pieces of ourselves like free samples at a supermarket, hoping that everyone who takes a bite will approve. We want to be liked, accepted, and seen as accommodating. We'll overserve to please others, even when it leaves us feeling drained and undervalued. But then comes a moment, or a series of moments, when we wake up and realize that giving too much just doesn't sit well with us anymore. Maybe it's maturity, or maybe we just get tired of feeling resentful, but we start to see the power in rationing out our energy.

Think back to a moment in your youth when you made a radical change, a time when you shifted from one version of yourself to another. For me, it was around age 13 when I went from having a complete hellscape of a teenage bedroom with clothes strewn everywhere and complete chaos in, on, and around my dresser to spending an entire day organizing it, turning chaos into something respectable. That moment wasn't just about tidying up; it was about deciding to live differently, even if I didn't have the language for it at the time.

Our boundaries and tolerances evolve, just like our taste buds. What worked for us back then, or what we put up with, might not work anymore. Consider how you navigate your relationships, friendships, and career. There may have been times when you bit your tongue to keep the peace or felt uncomfortable sharing your accomplishments because you worried about seeming "too much." We often follow unspoken rules we never consciously agreed to, making us feel trapped like we're being served a dish we didn't order but feel obligated to eat.

These unspoken rules can lead to internal conflict, causing us to shrink or accommodate, even when it doesn't feel true to who we are. We've been taught, directly or indirectly, that our needs should come second, or that being upfront about what we want makes us selfish. But what if we stopped worrying about looking selfish and started focusing on balance and accepting portions that make sense for us? What if expressing our desires openly could lead to deeper connections rather than tension? What if embracing our needs felt as natural as choosing a meal that satisfies us instead of one that leaves us hungry or unsatisfied?

I see people grappling with these questions more often as they get older. They wonder why they hold back, and they get frustrated with themselves for staying quiet or feeling guilty for their happiness. Sometimes, they've been so focused on being considerate or humble that they've lost sight of their own needs. It's like pouring your best energy into a meal no one appreciates, leaving you feeling drained and undervalued.

But boundaries aren't about building walls; they're about setting the right portions. They're about respecting ourselves enough to say, "This is not for me. This is what I need." *It's not selfish to be clear about what nourishes you, and it's perfectly okay to let go of what no longer satisfies.* Knowing when to pull back, when to engage, and when to walk away is part of finding that balance—a balance that allows you to live in alignment with your evolving self. It's like knowing that after ten years of snowboard vacations, I only want to do it for a few days and spend the rest of the trip reading, snowshoeing, or doing some other snow adventure—because my passion for the sport is not the same as Jeana's and that is okay.

So, how have your boundaries, desires, and tolerances shifted over time? Where do you hold back, and where do you give too much? Are you honoring your changing tastes, or are you still forcing yourself to accept things you've outgrown? There's no definitive answer, just the ongoing process of experimenting, adjusting, and finding the portions that work for you. Because, at the end of the day, life is about balancing the flavors, savoring what serves you, and letting go of the rest.

Sex Ed

One afternoon in sixth grade, with parental consent, we were split into two groups: boys in one classroom, and girls in another. It was sex ed day—or more accurately, reproduction day. This was when we learned the uncomfortable specifics of how babies are made. If I had to guess, most of us hadn't had "the talk" with our parents yet, even if we kind of knew the basics.

After several hours of watching childbirth videos and a slideshow presentation, we fled the room. Some of us were awkwardly giggling while others were silent, clutching our maxi pads as we merged into the hallway with the boys. Fast forward to eleventh grade—time for part two. This time, our health teacher covered STDs and pregnancy prevention, including a condom demonstration using a banana, and a warning not to flip a used condom inside out. Yes, apparently, that is a thing.

As a young woman going through puberty with everyone else, I intuitively understood that relationships followed a certain path, had consequences and that sex in some form was part of it. But like many young women, and probably young men too, I often danced with the trinity of: what I wanted, what I didn't want, and what I thought was expected of me.

By eleventh grade, we had all the stats and info about diseases and pregnancy. Yet, we were still trying to figure out how to set our own boundaries—if we even felt allowed to have them—and how to communicate and respect them. It takes time to realize you don't have to serve all the food at once, or even try everything on the table.

In her 2019 Netflix special, *Growing,* Amy Schumer talks about how we toughen little boys up so much that being tough becomes their way of showing affection. She shares examples like a boy knocking a book out of a girl's hand or teasing her, only for the girl to hear, "Oh, that means he likes you." This teaches the unconscious mind to equate poor treatment with affection, setting a low bar for future relationships.

In the Netherlands, their open approach to sexuality includes compulsory education beginning at age four, where they start to learn the basics of respecting each other's personal space and boundaries. A partnership between Rutgers University, the Netherlands Centre on Sexuality, and SOA Aids Netherlands created a transparent and clear age-appropriate curriculum that not only discusses the technical elements of sex, but covers topics like gender and relationships, consent, and encourages boys to express their feelings and needs while simultaneously teaching girls how to feel confident making their own choices surrounding sexuality without giving in to peer pressure. It further includes education for parents and encourages their awareness and participation in the school curriculum.

Resulting from its open, holistic discussion about sexuality and relationship dynamics, a 2020 Rutgers study reveals that 64% of Dutch men and women feel comfortable discussing sex and are confident stating their needs and desires. Furthermore, the Dutch have some of the lowest rates of teen pregnancy according to a 2020 report from Statistics Netherlands, known as the Centraal Bureau voor de Statistiek (Central Agency for Statistics). In fact, its pregnancy rate per 1,000 teenage girls ages 15-19 was about 7 times lower than that of the United States.

It seems that our initial introduction to sex education in school, focusing on reproduction and disease prevention, misses the mark because it is so much more. Culturally taboo and often hidden by a religious veil, young people are denied the holistic education that can be co-provided by school and the home. As a society, we fail to address the challenge of understanding and communicating personal boundaries, intentions, and desires which can be addressed at young ages. What we needed wasn't just information. We needed permission—to ask questions, to set boundaries, and to figure out who we were without shame.

Real education isn't just about preventing outcomes, it is about preparing people to know themselves, speak up, and make choices they can stand behind.

What About Me?

My friend Regina went on a fantastic cruise with her husband and another couple. Regina felt guilty because her best friend, Darla, couldn't afford the trip, so she didn't tell her. "I feel bad," she kept saying.

I asked, "So, you feel bad for accepting an invitation for a trip you've always wanted to take, with money you and your husband saved?" "You feel bad your best friend might be envious, even though she's the one who spends the most time with you?" Friends don't expect each other to miss out on life's joys just because they can't join in.

We talked about this a few times before the trip and Regina was wrecked because she had not yet shared her vacation plans with Darla— the secret burning her from the inside. With a head shake and a perplexed forehead wrinkle, I muttered, "Huh…So now you not only feel guilty about the trip but also guilty about keeping the secret?" "Yep. It's killing me," Regina said, "I even talked to my priest about it."

"And what did he say," I inquired. "Same thing. I have nothing to feel guilty about," Regina replied. "So, what is this feeling doing for you any-way?" I furthered. "Makes me feel bad that we are more financially stable," she acknowledged. I asked Regina to consider why she felt so guilty for being successful. She admitted that her best friend had always been sup-portive, but there was an unwritten loyalty pact between them since they were teens. It was the kind of pact we make as kids that promises we will share big adventures together for the rest of our lives—with no concept of our future financial situations or lifestyles.

Eventually, Regina told her best friend about the vacation, which led to weeks of ignoring the existence of the upcoming cruise and occasional passive-aggressive comments by Darla. In fact, before the trip, her best friend didn't mention it, and after, she didn't ask a word about how it was.

Of course, this bothered Regina, and we talked about how true friends want each other to be happy even if they can't be at every meal. But it doesn't mean they won't still feel a bit envious sometimes.

Eventually, thanks to some cocktails and Regina's husband, the door was opened for them to talk and air it all out. Her friend eventually came around and was excited to hear about some of the adventures.

If you're holding back good news or downplaying your joy because you feel guilty, *that's not kindness, it's shrinking.* Your happiness doesn't take anything away from anyone else and hiding it doesn't help them either. It's okay to enjoy what's good in your life. You don't have to apologize for it. Just stay compassionate.

Likewise, if people are hiding things from you or lying because they're afraid of how you'll react, that says something about the space you are creating—or it shows how they've learned to suppress their own joy. Being genuinely happy for someone else, even when you don't have the same, is one of the hardest and most generous things you can do. We're not all going to be served the same thing at the same time, but that doesn't mean we can't be glad someone at the table is getting something good. And it usually makes room for more of that in your own life.

Pianos & Presents

My friend Valerie's daughter had been playing piano for a few years. At first, she loved it—the challenge, the sound her fingers created when dancing across the keys, and the way her teacher's enthusiasm made each lesson feel like a personal triumph. But as time went on, her interest faded. Practice became a chore, and lessons were something to endure rather than enjoy.

One day, after yet another stalling tactic to avoid practicing, Valerie sat her down, "What's really going on?" she asked.

Her daughter hesitated, then finally confessed, "I just don't want to do it anymore." She said it was too much work for something she just didn't love.

Valerie understood. "Then it's time to tell your teacher."

That was met with immediate resistance. "But I don't want to upset her! She's so nice, and she loves the piano so much. I don't want her to think I don't care about everything she's taught me."

Valerie, always looking to empower her daughter, put the task of ending lessons under her daughter's control. She reminded her, "You don't have to be mean. Just be honest. She'll understand."

When the next lesson rolled around, Valerie's daughter seemed ready to have the conversation. But instead of telling the truth, she told her instructor that her parents thought lessons were getting too expensive.

Her teacher, a kind and generous woman, immediately responded, "If money's the issue, I'm happy to work something out. I'll lower my rate. I'd hate for you to stop."

Now stuck, Valerie's daughter stumbled over another excuse: "It's also school. I just have so much work. I don't have time to practice."

This went on for weeks, one excuse after another until her teacher finally understood what was really happening and let her go. "It's okay," she said. "You don't have to keep taking lessons if you don't want to."

When Valerie and her daughter got in the car after the final lesson Valerie asked, "Why didn't you just tell her the truth in the beginning? Wouldn't it have been easier?"

"Because I didn't want to hurt her feelings," she replied.

Haven't we all done this? We avoid saying what we really mean, thinking we're sparing someone's feelings when in reality, we're making things messier. Instead of being clear, we offer excuses, and the other person— trying to solve the problem we've created—keeps circling back, leaving us scrambling.

It reminds me of a gift I once received from a client. Tracy brought me a bottle of RumChata, a cream liqueur from Jamaica, something tied to her culture and heritage. I thanked her warmly and said I'd try it, but the truth was, I don't drink liqueurs. Rather than letting the bottle go to waste, I told her that after sampling it, I'd love for her to keep the bottle to enjoy with friends who would truly appreciate it. She was a bit surprised at my honesty while also appreciating that I did not want to waste it.

Tracy got to share her heritage while I honored my own truth. I wasn't rude, and I didn't pretend. Instead, there was space for both of us to feel good about the exchange.

In Valerie's daughter's case, her teacher likely felt hurt—not because she quit, but because the excuses signaled a lack of trust in their relationship, and also took up valuable time in her schedule that could have been given to other students. If her daughter had simply said, "I don't love it enough to put in the work," it might have stung, but it also would have allowed her teacher to understand and let go without the confusion.

This isn't just about piano lessons and gifts. It's about being honest, even when it feels uncomfortable. Maybe it's turning down a dinner invitation: *Thanks for thinking of me, but I don't feel comfortable with the group.* Or ending a relationship: *You're a great person; I just don't feel the connection I need.*

The truth, shared with kindness, is so much simpler. It saves time, energy, and emotional labor for everyone involved. And it allows others to meet you where you are, instead of trying to solve problems that don't really exist.

Perspective is everything. Valerie's daughter thought she was protecting her teacher by dodging the truth, but in reality, she was prolonging the inevitable and making it harder for both of them.

When you're honest about what you want or don't want, it's not just a kindness to yourself; it's a kindness to others. It lets them see you clearly, respect your boundaries, and move forward without unnecessary guesswork. So, the next time you feel tempted to dance around your truth, ask yourself: Am I really sparing someone's feelings, or am I just creating false problems for them to solve?

Hairy Subjects

Curiosity isn't the problem. It's how you bring it up.
There's a big difference between asking a genuine question and putting someone on edge. Some people come in strong. Others act like they're not even allowed to notice things. There's a middle ground and that's usually where real conversation happens.

I've always asked questions. I like understanding how people work, what they care about, and why they do the things they do. But I've learned that a lot of people hear a question and assume it's a critique. That's their filter, not mine.

Like one time, I asked someone why they kept a plant in a completely dark room. I wasn't judging their ability to care for a plant. I was honestly curious how the thing was still alive.

If I had said, "You know plants need light, right?"—that may have been interpreted as rude.

What I actually said was, "Hey, how does your plant do so well in here? Most wouldn't survive in such a dark space."

Same curiosity with a different tone.

And sometimes you need to give a little leeway depending on who is asking the question. Like kids. They don't think about tone or directness. For example, years ago, I cut off my long hair. A friend picked me up for lunch, and her 7-year-old daughter was with her. The second she saw me, she said, "Are you a boy now?"

I wasn't offended. She was seven. So, I asked, "What made you ask that?" She said, "Because boys have short hair."

Then I asked if she'd ever seen a boy with long hair. She nodded "yes."

I said, "Right. Just like that, I'm still a girl, I just have short hair." That was it. She understood and moved on. And even if she was trying to push buttons, something she was famous for, I did not react so it killed the fun.

Hair is one of those things people get weird about. A Black friend of mine used to joke that she had to protect her baby's head from white ladies constantly reaching out to touch his hair. We laughed because we both understood what was happening. Innocent curiosity, but a little too personal for a stranger. Similarly, when a white friend went to Nigeria on a volunteer trip, they told her ahead of time that people might want to touch her hair. And they did. They weren't being rude they were curious about something unfamiliar.

Another friend, Char, used to change her hair every few days. One day it was down to the middle of her back, the next it was short, and then it was something else entirely. I couldn't help but ask questions. How are extensions attached? What's the difference between plaits and braids? How long does it take?

Knowing me, she always answered but finally said, "Nicole, you can only ask me these questions. You can't ask other Black women about their hair like that."

With innocent confusion, I said, "Why not?"

She said, "They don't want people to know it's not theirs."

I looked at her and said, "Char. Come on. You had hair to your waist on Monday, and now it's barely brushing your shoulders. It's not exactly a secret."

We both laughed. But it made me realize that sometimes people aren't reacting to the question itself, but to what it brings up.

Sometimes people are not judging or shaming. They're just trying to understand something that's different.

I've had a ton of hair conversations at work and with friends, especially with women. We talk about volume, texture, age, hormones, extensions, all of it. Sometimes it is just surface level. Other times it's deeper. Conversations can be a little like seasoning—too bland and people feel unseen, too strong and they shut down. But when it's balanced just right, they'll tell you more.

Portals

I grew up with a basement as a young northerner. I no longer have one because my home in Florida is only seven feet above sea level, and it would be filled with water. So, if you've never seen a basement, there are two main types: the utilitarian kind where laundry is done, tools and boxes are stored, and the furnace glows; and the other kind, an alternate universe with all that plus a fully renovated living space.

This second type is where we teenagers hung out with friends or spent time while on home dates. As a teen, parents preferred us hanging out there instead of encouraging bedroom activities. Because somehow, the cloistered basement felt more public to them than a bedroom despite being accessed via staircase.

I had one long-term boyfriend in high school, and by "long-term," I mean six months. Otherwise, I just dated—a few dates here, a month or so there. Every time I hung out at a boy's place, the basement door felt like a portal.

As a young woman going through puberty, I was curious about sex but not ready to rush things with someone I was just getting to know. Plus, even if I was eager to move fast, I didn't want to be branded a "slut," which was worse than being called a "tease," but still better than being labeled a "prude."

So, every time I entered a portal, I assessed what I was willing to do, creating my own sexual boundaries in advance, figuring they might slip into the gray zone as I navigated the expected banter.

Why didn't we get guidance on navigating this real sexual coming-of-age, along with understanding the nuances of managing the awkward transition from platonic to romantic or sexual relationships? What we needed was open discussion as young men and women. We all already knew how to put the round piece in the circle hole from those shape sorter toys as kids.

Instead, boys learn to be the gas, and girls learn to be the brakes. An awkward tango of offense and defense. Boys feeling obligated to pursue, even if they're not really inspired. Girls feeling stifled for wanting sexual freedom, as if wanting it stripped them of value.

But we don't have to keep playing those old roles. As adults, we can unlearn any dynamic. We can talk honestly about what we want without shame, without pretending. We can say what we're craving, where our boundaries are, and what we're open to trying. It doesn't have to be all or nothing. Not everyone's ready for the full course.

Divorce

Years ago, while shopping with a friend, we passed an American Girl® doll store. Intrigued by the craze at the time, I wanted to go in to learn why. Having a young daughter herself, my friend explained how each doll represented a different era or persona, complete with a unique name, storyline, and timeline of experiences. The store, filled with dolls representing girls aged 8 to 11, also featured many accessories and a hair salon for the dolls and children; a blend of absurdity and brilliance.

All I could think of was how some adults were probably watching children play imagination games and started taking notes, bringing their concepts to life.

The oldest representation of dolls dates to 1854, with a storyline detailing life as an immigrant and working hard in school and on her family's farm. As I walked the store, each doll showcased the hardships of her era, and stories of resilience and hope; storylines that centered around topics like slavery, war, and the Great Depression.

Then I found her, the Gen X doll representing my birth decade of the 70's: Julie Albright, now part of the Historical Character Collection (gasp!). I couldn't wait to see her storyline.

Divorce. That was Julie's hardship.

Really? That was it? Then it struck me. I couldn't recall another little kid like me with not only a divorced, but single mother. According to sociologist W. Bradford Wilcox of nationalaffairs.com, in the older model of marriage, parents were supposed to stay together for the children to preserve their emotional well-being and protect their social and economic future. The newer soul-mate model, however, believes that if parents leave unhappy marriages, it protects the emotional well-being of the children, and they can replace absent fathers with other male role models.

Basically, there was a shift from viewing divorce as traumatic for children, to a pathway for personal growth and emotional well-being.

Yes, and thank you.

While my father was not a part of my life as an infant and toddler by my mother's choice, he was not a part of my life as I got older by my choice, despite my mother asking if I wanted to meet him periodically. I've been told he was a great craftsman. He was quick, smart, and very skilled. Unfortunately, he was a heavy drinker, and it led to his early death.

In my own life, divorce shaped my upbringing. My mother worked and completed her college education when I was young, allowing me to spend a great deal of time with my grandparents. Since I spent more time with grandparents than most children, it gave me a unique opportunity to learn about them, eventually understanding how they shaped my mother and her siblings, both of whom also acted as role models and safety outside the traditional nuclear family structure.

My mother was a part of the wave of women who decided that she wanted more for her life and that life was more than sticking out a bad relationship for the kids. Instead, she left for me and for her, showing me that boundaries and values are essential, that we are capable as individuals, and that there are people to lean into for help. Because of her decision, I was spared the anguish of alcoholism, yelling matches, and fear of an unpredictable home life.

Reflecting on my experiences, both personal and professional, I've witnessed the enduring physical, mental, and emotional scars of toxic family environments. It reinforces the importance of recognizing when a situation is harmful and having the courage to seek change rather than giving more and more hoping that it will fix everything. When we don't leave situations that are harmful or feel wrong, we need to look inside and ask ourselves why we continue to stay in circumstances that are unhealthy for us.

Blockbuster Night

Tired of manipulative and ambiguous dating rituals, I decided to flip the narrative during college. I had spent so many of my younger years repressing simple things that I did not want to limit any part of myself moving forward. I decided that I would do my best to live as authentic as possible, asserting my desires and boundaries, and accepting the discomfort that comes with the unfamiliar.

Occasionally, I pursued a boy I was interested in, who was often met with relief because as a good male friend once told me, "Getting rejected gets tiring since we always have to make the first move." If women were more empowered to own their space sexually and didn't wait to be courted men wouldn't need to make the first move so often. It's no surprise then, that when dating feels like cold calling and rejection is constant, getting a date turns into a numbers game.

By my mid-twenties, having long established that I valued truthful intentions, I had no problem being matter-of-fact, yet kind. Before Netflix and chill, we had Blockbuster nights. You would go to the store and rent your VHS tape for three days. Sometimes, being overzealous you might find yourself renting too many movies at once.

One Sunday night in the late '90s, I remember getting ready to settle in for the night with a movie due back by Monday. As I entered my living room the phone rang—it was a guy I was getting to know. "What are you doing tonight?" he asked. I told him I was getting ready to watch a movie which led him to invite me over to hang out and watch the movie at his place.

At first, I thought, sure that would be nice. Then it occurred to me, "So, are you inviting me over to watch the movie or because you want to hook up?"

"I mean we can see where the night takes us," he replied.

Got it. So, I said, "You know that you don't need to manipulate me right? If your goal is to hook up just tell me. I'm fine with that if I'm in the mood. But if you are inviting me over to watch a movie, which I really want to see on its last night of rental, then you barely let me watch it, I'm gonna be pissed."

"Ok," he replied, "I thought we could mess around tonight."

"Awesome. Thank you for being honest. Let me think about it and I'll call you back."

I considered my options for a few minutes then called him back for a rain check. I just wanted a chill movie night. What was great about that exchange was that moving forward, we were both clear about the real purpose or expectations each time we hung out.

These experiences were among the first where I learned to define the personal boundaries of relationships. It allowed both me and the other person to be comfortable with our desires and expectations, and to respond to each other appropriately. I realized I could ask for more of what I wanted, decline what I didn't, or suggest a modification to what I was being served. *Navigating all types of relationships is tough at times, but learning to listen and define your needs is essential when developing healthy and respectful relationships.*

And sometimes, you're just here for dessert, and that's fine, too.

Good Wine

When you feel good in yourself, the things you do reflect that, and what shows up in your life tends to follow. Too often, we try to patch up internal unhappiness with external stuff, hoping it'll fix the feeling. But it usually doesn't. It has to start from the inside.

After a client lets go of the unconscious baggage and limiting beliefs that have been holding them back during a "breakthrough session," one of the first things I ask of them is to create an avatar of themselves. And no, I'm not talking about video game characters or social media profile pictures. This is a personal avatar—a reflection of who they are at their core to ensure that their goals and the methods they use to reach them align with who they are.

The reason this is so important is simple: if who you are, what you do, and what you have are not aligned, you're going to feel out of place, like something's missing. This is why goal setting and goal getting often fail. You could have all the material things, but if they don't reflect your values, they won't bring you true satisfaction. It's like an endless retail shopping excursion where you try filling the emptiness of your being with what you have.

Think about it like this: if I told you that to make more money (have), you had to cheat or steal (do), you'd probably feel that it's wrong. That's the gut feeling of misalignment with your (being). I use this example a lot with clients who are working through career transitions or life changes. If you're constantly doing something that doesn't resonate with who you really are, it's like wearing shoes that are too small. You might be able to walk, but it's uncomfortable, and eventually, it's going to hurt.

In fact, depending on where you are in life, you've probably noticed a shift in your priorities. Early on in our careers, most of us focus on what we can have—the paycheck, the house, the car, the stuff. Then, there's often a point where we start craving more experiences, and want to do new things—travel, new hobbies, maybe even time to just enjoy life. Finally, many of us reach a stage where we want to focus on just being—being content, fulfilled, and at peace. It's a natural progression we follow, but what if we changed that approach?

I often tell clients that if they shift the order to *being, doing,* and then *having,* things start to feel more aligned. It's not about just getting things or ticking off achievements. It's about being who you truly are first, then doing things that reflect that, and finally, having the things that naturally follow. As time passes and your values change, so will your avatar. Who I was at 25 isn't who I am today, and the same will be true for you. And the key element is being okay with being you.

Much like a naturally gifted artist might follow the footsteps towards medicine in a family of doctors, people often inappropriately move along the path they think they should be doing based upon societal trends or long-standing familial expectations that may not match who they are.

Let me give you an example from the world of work because this misalignment can be really apparent in our careers. Picture someone who's an A+ worker. They value hard work and put in the hours, or maybe that's how they've always gotten their love and recognition cup filled. Now imagine them in a workplace that's more like a C+ environment—where the work ethic isn't as strong, and there's not a lot of appreciation or acknowledgment. What happens? That A+ worker keeps pouring themselves into the job, but it's like pouring expensive wine for someone who doesn't even care. You wouldn't do that, right? You'd switch to the average wine because there's no point wasting the good stuff on someone who doesn't appreciate it.

I've had friends complain about people who drink all their good wine without caring about it, and I tell them, "Well, why don't you just buy cheaper wine for those people who don't appreciate it like you so you can stop complaining?" The same goes for your energy. If you keep pouring your time, love, and commitment into a job (or a relationship, or anything really) that doesn't value it, you're going to feel drained. You either need to adjust what you're giving or find a new place that appreciates what you bring to the table.

You might find you are doing this in your own life. Are you working hard in a career where your efforts aren't recognized? Or in a relationship where you're giving and giving, but not getting much back? It's worth asking yourself how much longer you are willing to keep serving the biggest and best portions of you, and pouring your best energy into something or someone that doesn't appreciate it. Do you keep pouring because you are trying to fill everyone's cup? Because that often doesn't work and leads to resentment by both sides.

I see this especially with women because we tend to sacrifice a lot of ourselves for others—our families, our jobs, our communities. Sacrifice isn't necessarily a bad thing, but when you're constantly sacrificing your values, your time, and your energy without getting anything back, that's when it becomes a problem.

It's funny how we'll complain about wasting material things, like good wine, but when it comes to wasting our own energy and joy, we just keep pouring. Why do we do that?

Maybe it's time to reflect on why self-sacrifice is so acceptable. If you want to be around people and circumstances that appreciate your best qualities, then you need to get rid of the stuff filling that space and seek out environments that align with who you are. Whether that's a better workplace, a stronger circle of friends, or even new hobbies that fulfill you.

I work with a lot of high-achieving women, and something I've seen over and over again is this tendency to keep pushing ourselves to prove something—at work, home, anywhere for that matter. We work harder and harder, hoping that our efforts will finally be acknowledged or rewarded, but when the environment doesn't match our values, that acknowledgment often never comes. It's frustrating, exhausting, and it feels like you're on a hamster wheel.

Imagine being in a space where you're appreciated. Where what you bring to the table is seen and valued. You're not walking around trying to prove yourself all the time. You just get to be you. It would shift how you move through your day, how you connect with people, and how you feel about yourself.

At the end of the day, this process of alignment—of bringing together who you are, what you do, and what you have, isn't just about being happier at work or in your relationships—it's about living a life that feels fulfilling and authentic to you. It's about being able to look at your life and say, "Yeah, this feels right." So, ask yourself what you really want in your life. And are your current actions in alignment with who you are at your core, or are they just fulfilling an expectation?

Maybe it's time to stop pouring the good wine for people who don't appreciate it and start saving it for those who do.

4ᵀᴴ COURSE

Life isn't going to stay mild. No matter how much we'd like to avoid it, the spicy moments that make us squirm, sweat, stumble, or want to run tend to be the ones that shape us the most. Discomfort isn't a punishment; it's a mirror, reflecting back what we need to face. Many years ago, I heard a lecturer describe growth as the uncomfortable process of peeling back the layers of an onion—you may not want to do it, but it is necessary and you're gonna cry the whole time. Like an onion, discomfort forces us to peel away the layers of who we thought we were, revealing a version of ourselves that's stronger, wiser, and if we let it, a little more at peace. *Discomfort disrupts our rhythm and challenges us to deal with it. It makes us ask how hard we will hold on to the way things were, or if we will let this discomfort shape us into something new.* It's realizing that every couple longing for the way things "used to be when we started dating" is in trouble because life is not static but a winding journey.

Discomfort isn't an intruder; it's a catalyst. It shakes you from the familiar and forces you to take a closer look at the habits, beliefs, and routines you've been clinging to. It's like finally noticing that the turkey on white bread sandwich you've been making your whole life is no longer interesting; it's just safe and easy. And maybe all it needs is some fresh thyme and herbed olive oil to liven it up. At first, it feels unnecessary, even wrong, like using mayo instead of butter to grill your cheese sandwich or adding a slice of tomato. But then you realize it's not about letting go of the familiar; it's about finding new ways to spice up your current life.

Growth doesn't happen when we are comfortable. It shows up in the roadblocks and failed attempts and the moments when you're not sure if you're doing it right. After more than two decades of working with clients in various formats, I can attest to this. It's in the decision to say "yes" and try even when it feels easier not to, leaning into all the reasons it won't work instead. Discomfort has this sneaky way of teaching you what you're capable of—not in some grand, sweeping way, but in the small, everyday moments that challenge your assumptions about yourself and the world. It's like a Floridian who suddenly realizes they are spending too much time worrying about losing power during a hurricane rather than preparing for it and making do without the creature comforts we've become used to.

Discomfort has a way of breaking down and clearing out the clutter—ego, fear, self-doubt—and making room for the real work to begin. It teaches us to lean in, to trust ourselves, and to see challenges not as obstacles but as invitations to grow. I think about all the times I have resisted something, clinging to what's safe and predictable. And each time I stopped fighting and started leaning in there was a shift. It's taking a leap to move across the country, to quit your job, to leave a relationship—to leave what is familiar for what is fulfilling. That's when the transformation happens. It's not about seeking out hardship, but about being willing to face it when it comes. Too often we run from or around obstacles, when in fact, those obstacles were put there to make us learn something about ourselves.

Because even the smallest moments of bravery like trying something new, admitting you don't have all the answers, apologizing, or letting go of what's no longer working, can expand the way you see yourself and what you're capable of. Coaching clients always thank me for helping them get through a loop they've been stuck in. But I remind them that it was always them—their desire to let go of the familiar and step into something uncomfortable for a chance at a life they never thought could exist for them.

Discomfort burns. It forces you to wash down what no longer serves you, leaving room for something better. It's about accepting that life will bring you a cabinet of spices whether you're ready for them or not. And you get to decide what to do: to season the life you're building or to let it overwhelm you.

With enough distance, pain starts to turn into perspective. It doesn't erase what happened, but it helps make sense of why it mattered. You don't have to love every hard moment, and you don't have to pretend it's easy. But when you stop running from discomfort, you'll find it's not just a challenge, it's an opportunity. To learn. To grow. To inspire. And to become someone you didn't know you could be.

Metabolife

As an 18-year-old in my first year of college, I gained the "Freshman 15" by the time I went home for winter break. No longer an athlete and having discovered beer and 3 A.M. burritos, it wasn't too surprising. When I saw my uncle during winter break, he looked at me playfully and said, "Well, I see you're not starving." It wasn't intended to be a mean comment since he enjoyed his pasta, too, but it reinforced something I already knew: I needed to make a choice about how I wanted to live my life. So, instead of spiraling out of control, I made choices that made me feel good. I chose fewer late-night burritos, better foods by day, and fewer beers, opting for more vodka-based drinks instead because I heard liquor had fewer calories and could get you drunk with less. What can I say, I was a young college gal.

By my junior year in college, I was shockingly balanced in my well-being—navigating decent food choices for a 20-year-old now that I was living in a house versus the dorm and incorporating strength and cardio sessions at the newly built fitness center. But life was still pretty chill at that point.

After finishing undergrad, life was a blur of movement. I worked multiple jobs, finished my graduate degree in one year, and pushed myself to stay as lean and fit as possible with the knowledge I had at the time. I thrived in the go-go-go lifestyle, always juggling responsibilities and opportunities. But as I look back, I see how I was caught in a cycle, controlling every moment so I could fit it all in.

I wasn't just surviving; I was genuinely enjoying my life and took pride in my ability to burn the candle at both ends. I loved weekends when I could go clubbing with friends, and the feeling of house and trance music running through me. Music and dancing weren't escapes for me, they made me feel alive and vibrant. It was a way to release all the energy from my week, to let loose and exist in the moment, especially after the long hours of work, school, and daily cardio workouts which mirrored the intensity with which I danced.

I lived a carefree life. After all, I was single and in my twenties. I flew to Chicago one weekend to visit a friend and to dance, and on a different weekend I drove eight hours to New York City alone after work, just to experience their epic club scene for a couple of days. And while that kind of spontaneity might seem reckless, it was part of the fearless and free way I lived back then, exploring almost anything I wanted to about myself and my experiences. When you're in full-throttle mode, fear doesn't really register in the same way. I didn't make too many reckless choices, but there were certainly a few along the way.

But in the midst of that high-energy life, I also developed habits that were less about freedom and more about control. I was what you'd call an exercise bulimic. I made sure that every calorie I consumed was mostly burned off during the one-hour cardio sessions I would cram in during the two-hour lunch breaks I negotiated. Every day was about burning, burning, burning. According to the elliptical where I read most of the case studies required for my MBA classes, I burned 800 to 1000 calories per hour. If you have ever done an hour of cardio, you understand the speed and intensity required to achieve those numbers. From a cardiovascular standpoint, I was like a powerful locomotive and the Energizer Bunny wrapped into one. I didn't really do strength training because my limited understanding of fitness kept me focused on the calories churning on the machine. It was a relentless cycle.

This extreme pattern of control extended beyond my exercise routine. I didn't drink alcohol, didn't eat sugar or starch, focusing only on vegetables, protein and coffee. I became so strict that my coworkers eventually noticed. After the first office bagel day that I skipped my coworkers told me I needed more carbs because I was irritable. They were right, but I was too focused on maintaining this idea of control over my body and my habits. Eventually, my irritability subsided.

At that time, a now-banned weight loss supplement hit the market—Metabolife, a loosely tested ephedra-based product. In my drive to stay lean and in control of my body, I started taking it. I was also drinking tons of coffee and limited water, thinking I needed the energy to keep up with my lifestyle. What I didn't realize was that my body was crying out for help. One day at work, after taking Metabolife and my usual excess of caffeine, my heart was racing so fast that my coworkers could literally see it beating through my chest. I felt nauseous, lightheaded, and scared. I was severely dehydrated. My coworkers rummaged through my desk drawers, found the pills, and threw them away like emptying a drug addict's stash. Then two of them drove me and my car home while I managed to not vomit in the backseat from the nausea. It was enough of a wake-up call to stop taking Metabolife, but at that point, I still wasn't fully ready to let go of my need to control everything.

A year later when I moved to Florida, that illusion of control really shattered. My routine had ended, I had too much free time in my day while looking for jobs, and the pull of the sun and beach overpowered my interest in cardio. Plus, I no longer had the necessary case studies to entertain me for an hour of grinding on a machine. I gained 18 pounds in just six weeks, something I like to share when I talk about the interconnectedness between nutrition and fitness.

Previously, I was burning more than just fat. I was losing lean body mass and my body's ability to burn calories efficiently on its own. I felt completely powerless. It was one of the most unsettling experiences of my life because it made me realize that unless I was laser-focused and on point nearly 100% of the time, my body would spiral. At that point, no matter what I did or how hard I tried, it was clear I was squeezing wet soap. The more I tried to control the situation the farther my goals drifted.

For the first time, I had to surrender.

Letting go was terrifying. After years of managing every calorie, every workout, and every detail, the idea of surrendering felt like I was giving up entirely. When fitness and coaching clients come to me today, believing I don't know what it is like to be scared, to let go and do something against all they have known I share this story. Like them, I needed to learn a new strategy even if it felt unfamiliar, scary, and would be slow-paced.

I had to trust the process.

In that surrender I found something far more valuable—balance. I realized that my body wasn't something to control or fight against; it was something to listen to and work with, so I began combining strength training and cardio, and learned about nutrition. Over time, the weight came off, not because I forced it to, but because I found a new approach—a sustainable, balanced way of living that respected my body rather than punishing it.

That shift wasn't just about fitness; it was a different approach to life in general. I had spent so much time trying to control every aspect of my life, but I realized that letting go and finding balance was far more effective. This lesson became a foundational part of how I coach others today. Whether it's in fitness, personal development, or professional growth, the underlying patterns are often similar.

Too often we look at people with an extreme focus on their fitness and believe they have it all under control. I once had a conversation with a friend that illustrates this very idea. She was obsessed with extreme workout programs with names like "Insanity" and "Cardio Freak." She'd go all-in for weeks, pushing herself to the limit, and then crash, doing nothing for months. Meanwhile, her husband was struggling with bouts of binge drinking. She saw herself as focused on fitness and well-being, and him as someone who was escaping into alcohol.

One day during a phone conversation I pointed out that they were both using their outlets to manage stress and emotions. Their behaviors may have looked different, but underneath, they were both responding to similar emotional needs—one by trying to control, and the other by disappearing. I suggested she ask her husband what he is feeling when he slips back into alcohol and that she might realize it is like what she is feeling when she launches into a new workout program. She did ask him, and to her surprise, his feelings were very similar to her feelings.

Whether it's exercise, food, alcohol, or even work, we all develop patterns to manage our emotional states. *The trick is recognizing when those patterns stop serving us or begin to run our lives.* You may even find yourself in and out of these patterns.

These experiences have given me an education so I can better help people today. I guide them in recognizing the patterns they've created—whether it's around food, exercise, work, or relationships—and help them make conscious choices that align with who they really are. It's not about rigid control, nor is it about letting everything fall apart. It's about balance. It's about finding the strategies that work, and more importantly, recognizing when the old patterns no longer serve you.

One of the most important lessons I've learned and that I pass on to others is that letting go isn't about giving up. It's about gaining perspective. When I finally let go of my obsessive need to control my body, I discovered a healthier, more sustainable way to live. It wasn't immediate, and it wasn't easy, but it was worth it. And that's what I help others find: the balance between effort and surrender, between action and acceptance. So, what patterns are you holding onto? Are they serving you, or are they keeping you stuck? Imagine what would it feel like to let go, even just a little, and find a new way forward.

Life will always have moments of chaos and spice and trying to control everything will only leave you feeling more overwhelmed. But if you can recognize the patterns that aren't serving you and make conscious choices to shift toward balance, you'll find a new sense of peace. It's not about perfection; it's about alignment—making choices that resonate with who you are and what you truly need.

Open Road

Running was never my thing. I would go so far as to say that I severely disliked it. Prior to college, my experience with running was limited to punishment during sports practices or the occasional sprint around bases in softball. Everything changed freshman year when I met a cross-country runner who would become a lifelong friend. At that point I was an athlete without a sport so somehow, I got roped into running with her.

It started with a vague promise of a warmup run. At 18, I didn't ask enough questions and assumed it would be short, less than a mile. Little did I know that we'd be running three miles. If you are not accustomed to distance running it might as well have been a marathon. Thankfully, my friend was forgiving in pace and stopped to let me get air as the cramps twisted in my gut each time we ran.

I complained incessantly at first, resisting every step, yet somehow managing to continue. I was way out of my comfort zone. She wanted a running buddy, and I was stubborn enough to keep going despite the burn in my legs and lungs, and lack of cardiovascular fitness.

It wasn't until I stopped fighting, complaining, and focusing on the difficulty of this new sport that I opened myself to improvement. As I learned proper running techniques, over time my complaints turned into controlled breathing, the cramps faded, and I learned to run efficiently. Sometimes I even ran on my own.

By the end of freshman year, I missed team sports. Since I had learned to run, I decided to join the women's rugby club. Like running, rugby was unfamiliar, but I knew I could learn a new sport. Running taught me that. Plus, if you don't know anything about rugby know this: you run, a lot, and hopefully fast. I would have never joined the rugby club if I did not already have a baseline of cardiovascular fitness which running had given me.

By junior year I was running on my own with regularity but that faded over time.

More than a decade after I first learned how to run, I was in a new state, working in fitness, and decided to take up martial arts. I had no idea that running was a requirement to earn a black belt. I had to run two miles in less than 16 minutes.

I still grumbled about running. I complained about my knees, my lungs, and the heat. I even considered faking an ankle injury every Saturday that we had to run a mile after class when I was in cycle for my black belt.

Then I gave in like I had sixteen years earlier. I decided to stop resisting, eventually accepting both its benefits and necessity. Instead of fighting, I leaned in. I couldn't change the situation, so I changed myself. Running became integral to my sparring conditioning, and martial arts enhanced my running stamina.

I kept running after I earned my black belt, three to five miles a few times per week. Five months later I decided to run a half marathon, diving in once again with no specific training. This time to see if I could. I even pulled it off with a pretty good time. My running journey taught me this: don't fight discomfort, use it. Whether it's running, martial arts, or anything unfamiliar, the willingness to adapt and keep going can lead to something surprisingly satisfying.

Don't Be Weird About It

I was on a cruise when I spotted a woman wearing these incredible hand-painted Dr. Martens boots. I couldn't help but compliment her on them. As we chatted, she mentioned they were the only shoes that worked well with her blade. *That's* when I realized she had a prosthetic leg. I hadn't noticed before because I was too focused on the boots. So, I asked, "If you don't mind me asking, was that something you were born with or from an injury?"

She gave a slight nod and said, "Shark attack."

Wow!

She explained that she lost her leg while surfing off the coast of Australia. While sitting on her surfboard near the boat, a great white shark grabbed her and pulled her under. It was an incredible story of her friends diving off their boards into the water to, as she described, "fight the shark for me."

They got her to the surface, on the boat, tied her leg, and dashed to shore quickly, which saved her life.

We talked about her recovery and how her stump kept changing size, how grateful she was that the amputation was below the knee, and how she'd recently gone surfing again. She shared her experiences as normally as she may have shared another part of her life story.

Before we parted ways, she said, "Thanks for just having a normal conversation. Most people get weird."

My pleasure.

Another time, at the gym, I noticed a guy with two prosthetic legs. He saw me glance over, and I smiled. I said, "So... did you make yourself taller?"

He laughed and replied, "Yeah, by two inches."

We ended up talking about our workouts, life, and eventually, how he lost both legs in separate incidents. It was a regular conversation—not focused on his prosthetics, but they were part of the dialogue.

These encounters made me realize that people who've been through significant challenges choose how to carry themselves. Both people had a certain grace and maturity. They've faced adversity and come out the other side, not seeking pity but connection as just another person.

Some people want to be noticed for what's missing. *Most people want to be seen for what's still there.*

It's not about making their experiences the focal point but acknowledging them as part of who they are. You don't need to pretend not to notice or avoid the topic. Just be genuine, ask respectfully if appropriate, and engage in a normal conversation.

Next time you encounter someone with a visible difference, don't be weird about it. Treat them like any other person. Because they are. They're just bringing their unique dish to the table.

Spicy & Sweet

During the decline of my relationship in my thirties, I learned a lot about myself, other people, and my participation in relationships. If you can imagine a vase filled with pebbles and water, I often describe myself as the water. I want my partner to fill the vase as much as they can with their pebbles, and I'll fill the space in between. You can't fill the space for someone else. In fact, trying to just creates more of it.

That said, I don't want only a quarter of the vase filled with pebbles. I'm looking for some semblance of equality. Over time, I've become more mindful of my role, especially when it starts to look like parenting. I am, after all, a caretaker of well-being. I can navigate my life, my partner's life, and our life. But I don't want to.

The demise of that relationship years ago was obvious. She had taken a new, high-stress job, and it completely shifted our dynamic. Our time together changed. The way we interacted changed. Then came the "friend" from work—someone she could lean on in ways I was told I wouldn't understand. The writing wasn't just on the wall, it was spray-painted across it. Our close friends saw it. I saw it. She didn't.

If you can't own your stuff, you're lying to yourself and everyone around you. Most people don't want to see the parts of themselves they can't yet admit exist in themselves. That's the shadow—part of a person they hide, deny, or disown.

By the time our relationship officially ended, I was already in full-focus growth mode. I was starting to blossom as a person and frankly, I knew it was ending. I wasn't just trying to understand her, I was learning about myself, too. Many people think therapy is a last-ditch effort because they wait until they are out the door emotionally. They see it as the end, not a tool for real connection. I saw it as education.

At the beginning of my next relationship—with my current wife—I told Jeana, "At some point, I'll probably ask you to go to therapy. Not because we're falling apart, but because I love you. And we'll probably get stuck somewhere, and I'll want help working through it." She bristled. Like many, she saw therapy as the end. I explained that I see it as another tool to make things better.

Imagine how any relationship could improve, even the one with ourselves if we just admitted we don't have all the answers. Still, for all the insight I was gaining, the end of that relationship hit me harder than I expected. Even though I had seen it coming, I felt like I was standing there holding a ball of unraveling yarn with no way to stop it. It felt unfair even though I had been unhappy, too. My ego was clawing and scratching, and my dreams were volatile. I felt unstable, a little crazy, and very much not in control. I'm grateful I went through that part. It gave me insight into how it must feel for people who live in that space all the time.

I still remember the day I decided to let go. I was looking out of my bedroom window. I was tired of letting something outside of me dictate how I felt. I needed to change my lens. Rather than carrying the burn of a broken ego, I decided to feel gratitude for her. For showing me how she navigated stress. For helping me learn about my own patterns. For teaching me something even if she didn't know she was doing it.

It's natural to want someone to change for you. We hope a parent gives up alcohol so they can show up when we are kids. We hope our partner chooses us over work or other people. But in the end, it's about *them*, not us. What we can control is how we set boundaries and what we bring into a relationship.

That breakup showed me my capacity for growth, and eventually, for forgiveness. Just like I remind my clients: forgiveness doesn't take time. It takes a decision. It's the preamble to the decision that takes forever.

Self-awareness is where it starts. You need to know who you are—the sweet and the spicy. You have to own it. The moments that burn? They teach us resilience, *if we let them*. And sometimes, letting go and choosing gratitude is what opens the door to real healing.

Though painful, that breakup turned out to be one of the best things that ever happened to me. Once I stopped focusing on what was happening *to* me and started asking what was happening *because* of me, everything shifted. I felt energetically connected to things around me in a way I hadn't before. I opened myself to new people, new experiences, and a deeper level of empathy and understanding.

It all funneled into my work—into how I coach, how I listen, and how I guide others through their own stuck places. *Growth isn't about being unbreakable. It's about choosing to transform, even when it hurts.* Though it wasn't easy to digest, like an unexpected course on a tasting menu, it ended up giving me something I didn't know I needed.

Unraveled

I was a particularly shy little girl who eventually became a bit bossy, letting the adults and kids around me know how to play a game or when it was time to move on. I like to say that I simply took the lead. Being an only child there was no one else who was going to initiate activity so I learned how. As I got older and middle school hit, I suffered the customary self-confidence issues a young person may have. In my case, however, it manifested as an inability to speak out loud for any length of time.

Imagine for a moment, a time in school where you had to read from your textbook out loud, each student taking a paragraph. The class reading as a collective one-by-one.

I recall a very specific day in Spanish class freshman year of high school. I was in the middle of a row near the door. Mr. Taylor asked us to read aloud, starting with the other side of the room. As the students read seamlessly, one-by-one, and my paragraph approached I became increasingly nervous. Finally, it was my turn. As I began to speak my eyes glossed over, my voice shook and cracked, and I began to unravel. I pushed on to the best of my ability, lost in my nerves and then my embarrassment because I was in full internal meltdown.

It was clear that I was suffering with each stuttered and stalled word. Barely halfway into my paragraph, however, it came: the silent save. Without an attempt to encourage me or any other scene, Mr. Taylor simply asked the next student to pick up where I had left off. I looked at him with eyes that said, "thank you" and he gave me a subtle nod of acknowledgment.

This was not the first time I suffered through reading out loud, but it was the worst experience. I felt foolish, and incapable, and it brought unwanted attention. I couldn't understand why it was so hard for me, but the extreme discomfort told me I had to figure it out.

Consider all the times you might have been wrecked by something. What did you do? Did you keep suffering? Avoid it? Or figure out how to overcome it?

Fortunately, I was blessed with the ability to see possibility and a stubbornness that tells me I can figure it out. I knew that I had to get over my fear of speaking in front of people. With years of schooling ahead of me, I knew public speaking would continue to haunt me. The following term I took a speech class as an elective.

I remember it being a very small class, which was perfect. Most of us were nervous, some were just filling their schedule. But all of us were required to create various types of small speeches: convincing, funny, and informational. While the main purpose of the class was to teach us how to craft different types of speeches, I used it as immersion therapy, the kind of technique that forces you to confront your fears head-on to realize you will survive. A little like trying raw oysters for the first time.

Fortunately for my coaching clients, I use a less in-your-face technique to help them release phobias and traumas so they don't actually need to re-live an experience to move past it. For most people, however, embracing challenges, like taking a speech class to overcome a fear of public speaking, can lead to personal growth and the ability to help others overcome their fears.

By senior year I had become a formidable student of Spanish and could read aloud in class with no problem. I had become more comfortable in my skin. Now in my sixth year learning the language I had a good grasp of its grammar and vocabulary and felt confident with my accent for a non-native speaker. Instead of Mr. Taylor, I now had Señora Anderson as a teacher. While Mr. Taylor had a more passive style of encouragement, Sra.

Anderson was more pushy, often exposing us to competitions and honors class opportunities.

As one of her most promising students, she encouraged me to participate in a language competition at Youngstown State University that year. Of the students who showed interest in the event I was chosen to represent the school in, you'll never guess, extemporaneous speaking. This meant that I had to outline and loosely prepare a three to five-minute speech about a topic to be delivered in front of a panel of judges and my peers.

I won second place.

What if I didn't unravel in class years earlier? I would not have been motivated to take speech class. Mr. Taylor's silent save was what I needed at that time, and Sra. Anderson was the nudge I needed during my senior year.

Consider the moments that made you feel helpless. Did they silence you, or become the start of something new? When we choose to embrace hard experiences and learn from them, we remind ourselves just how much we're capable of.

Awkward

It's been two decades since my friend Molly's daughter died. She was a toddler and her only child. One day we were talking, and I asked her how she feels when Mother's Day comes around. She said she's healed a lot and has found ways to move forward. Then I asked her if anyone ever talks about her daughter anymore. She said, "Not really." Most people avoid it. They're afraid to bring her up, like it'll reopen something.

So I asked her, "Is that good for you?"

She paused and said she had mixed feelings. On one hand, "it's easier not to have to manage other people's reactions." But on the other, not talking about it means she doesn't get many chances to share what her daughter was like, or what that experience really meant.

I told her I've noticed that people who are uncomfortable with their own emotions tend to be even more uncomfortable with other people's. So instead of being present, they dodge. And that silence creates even more distance.

Now when people ask Molly if she has kids, she just says no. It's simpler.

I get it in a different way. For years after 9/11, I hated telling people my birthday.

"Oh my god, I'm so sorry."

"Wow. That must be hard."

"I could never celebrate on that day."

And I'd be sitting there thinking...it's just my birthday. It didn't become a national tragedy because of me. I didn't need people to grieve when they found out about my date of birth.

Eventually, I'd just say something like, "It was my day first," and keep it moving.

I don't carry trauma about my birthday. But people would project all this emotion onto it. What should have been a simple question— "When's your birthday?"—suddenly became a moment. And sometimes I just wanted to give an answer and have it received like anyone else's.

Molly's story is much deeper than mine. But I think we both learned something similar: people mean well, but a lot of them don't know how to sit with something that makes them uncomfortable. So, they avoid it. Or they overreact.

Silence doesn't erase a story it just leaves someone holding it alone. It doesn't take a perfectly crafted response. Sometimes all people want is *to not have to hold your discomfort and theirs at the same time.*

It's like tasting a dish because it's special to the person who offered it. You don't need to love it. You just need to be willing to try it.

Capable

A: "Will you please descale the coffee maker today?"
B: "I don't know how."

B: "I did something to my iPhone, can you fix it?"
A: "Probably. Have you tried to find a solution online yet?"
B: "No, I'm not good at that stuff."

A: "Can you make dinner tonight, please."
B: "You know I can't cook."

B: "I have to take my car in for service, the "I" is lit up on my dashboard."
A: "You mean the tire pressure light?"
B: "I don't know. How do you know that?"
A: "Because I've looked it up before."

We live in a world that keeps serving grilled cheese thinking: simple, familiar, and low effort. As an empowerment and growth coach, I am often struck by how quickly people reassign power, lose it, or reject it out of simple disinterest. In the 1800's Thomas Jefferson equated knowledge with power, safety, and happiness. The reality is that for many young people, their power bucket was not filled with independence, choice or trust in the way childhood development specialists recognize as good for a child's confidence. As adults, this sometimes parlays into equating disempowerment as an opportunity to get attention and affection, yet for others, they emotionally default to their inabilities or lack of knowledge. It's almost like believing that since the power bucket was never filled, it has an invisible lid on it—low confidence or sometimes mere disinterest acting as the lids.

Growing up as an only child, I often shadowed the adults in my family. Without siblings to play with, I constantly sought out new challenges, trying to mimic the adults around me. Wherever they went, I followed, asking "why" and demanding to be taught whatever was happening. I also slipped under the radar with secret "experiments" and snooping. My quest for attention also filled my power bucket with knowledge, pride and confidence. Though I may have been internally motivated to fill my bucket, it was the adults around me that allowed it.

My grandpa's basement workshop and the garage were like playgrounds, filled with tiny baby food jars of screws, washers, and anything else Grandpa thought worth saving. There were plenty of broken-down pizza boxes, too, because "you never know when you're going to need a good piece of cardboard," he would say. This Depression-era mentality taught me how to repurpose, while upstairs I learned to cook pasta, meatballs, homemade sauce, and an iceberg lettuce salad for a family of five for only $5.99.

For whatever reason, one of my fondest memories is "helping" my uncle in the driveway. When I was very young, he lived in an apartment so if he needed to work on his car, to my grandparents' he went. Anytime he worked on the car I would pick up tools to assist in my own unhelpful way, with all the confidence of a toddler yelling, "I do, I do!"

I often tell the story of how he would give me a long bolt and a box of nuts, and a very important task: to put as many nuts on the bolt as possible, a job that kept me busy and out of trouble as I sorted through the box to find the nuts that fit. When I finished, I'd get praised for my skill. Then, I would need to remove the nuts and find a new set of nuts to fill the bolt.

When I was age five my mom's boyfriend, Craig, moved in with us. Craig often asked me to show him how strong I was, gesturing with a traditional biceps flex. The importance of strength eventually became one of my values. By nine he taught me how to drive a snowmobile and ATV, and I learned the hard way about the importance of standing clear when someone is casting their line while fishing. That's when I learned how to cut the barb off a fishing lure before pulling it out of a thumb. My thumb. Ouch! Fishing also taught me that boating bores me and I get seasick. We are not going to enjoy everything life gives us to taste.

I credit my family for teaching me almost anything I wanted, leaning into toys and tasks that I had an aptitude for, and give credit to the era. Having my formative years in the 80's was a different time. We stayed home alone, babysat infants before we were in double digits, drank from the hose, used the oven or stove at an early age, and rode bicycles without helmets. By the time I was ten, I learned to set my grandma's hair every week after she broke her shoulder and could no longer do it herself. That was around the same time Craig learned that I had good hand-eye coordination and could throw, which started my participation in team sports.

As an 80's child, I was given a lot of freedom and space to explore, something that seems to have been lost with younger generations. My family, happy to keep me out of their hair, would assign me tasks to figure out or teach me something new. Gifted with leftover orange yarn and a crochet hook, Grandma taught me a few basic stitches. Periodic crocheting kept me occupied for hours at a time. I even used my new skills to make Grandma a hideous cigarette pack holder which successfully held her Benson & Hedges and lighter, at least for a few days. Other times, I would make "volcanoes" in the backyard by mixing vinegar and baking soda to create a foamy eruption. My "lava" had a red-speckled hue, thanks to my secret raid of the spice drawer. I got yelled at often as you might imagine. In my youth it seems I asked for a lot more forgiveness than permission.

My curiosity and desire to help often led to memorable, and sometimes hazardous, experiments, too. Around age 12, I decided to deep clean my grandparents' first-floor powder room as a surprise. The real surprise, however, was when I learned that the ammonia, bleach, and vinegar mixture I created was toxic. I had watched Grandma clean with all of them at some point so I figured blending them together would be an even better cleaning solution.

Talk about growing through a spicy experience. As I cleaned the small room, I took breaks because the vapor burned my eyes and stifled my breathing. Its harshness reinforced that it must have been a good cleaning agent, I thought! It didn't take long for the gas to linger to where my grandma sat in the living room. Her frantic yelling and the speed with which she got to me told me I had made a big mistake. There was no Google to look up how to make a cleaning solution, and I wanted it to be a surprise, so I didn't ask what to mix. That toxic lesson helped me realize that part of learning is knowing when to ask for help, too.

Whether at my mom's or grandparents' house it was my hive. Me, a busy bee, buzzing from one thing to another. In our early days of dating, my wife once gave me a gift with a note that said "Tinker, tinker, my little thinker." Some things don't change. But they can if you want them, too. What would you do if no one ever told you that you couldn't? Do you encourage the people around you to figure things out for themselves?

I never had a list of regular chores to do as a kid because I wanted to do them to fill space. That doesn't mean I was not asked or told to do something. I cannot think of something I did not have my hand in as a child, and I was never told I was not capable in the subtle ways that children often hear. "That is for boys." "This is for girls." "Only big kids can do that." If anything, I was told how to do something better or that I needed to learn. Sometimes I did need a stern warning or a well-earned punishment. I met the backside of the wooden spoon plenty of times, which I had to deliver to the punisher in advance of the spanking as a warning shot to me. I made my choices.

Around age 13 I learned what a double boiler was, and how to make one with two pots. What preceded that education was my experiment making candles. I used to melt new candles to make my own in Styrofoam cups, a hobby that didn't sit well with the adults. Eventually, I was given an old aluminum pot and taught how to make a double boiler so I did not burn wax into the pot, instead using steam as heat. I experimented with candle layers, wicks, and different techniques. This hobby didn't turn into a candle-making career, but it did keep my hands and mind from being idle. Years later, my wife would ask, "When do we get our kitchen back?" as I experimented with making homemade essential oil-fragranced goat milk soaps for clients. Creating things for people brings me immense joy and pride. So, for me, knowledge is also happiness.

Even now, I still run a quick cost-benefit analysis before I try something new. It's like tossing a balled-up receipt toward the trash; if I miss, I've got to get up anyway, so no real loss. It's a balance of *not careless* with *not afraid to try.* You don't attempt some complicated recipe for a holiday dinner if it's your first time cooking. You either test it beforehand, pick something simpler, or be prepared to order takeout and move on. Either way, you learn.

I've realized I'm a jack of many trades and a master of none. As an entrepreneur and solo business owner, that's been incredibly useful. These days, information is everywhere. There's very little you can't learn if you're willing to look. Behavior change is hard sometimes, and it isn't always easy to learn something new, but you can if you choose to. Most of the time it's not impossible, just uncomfortable.

I've failed plenty of times, but mostly I've learned how to do things better or realize it is way beyond my level of ability. That's perspective. And if "I don't know how" is just code for "I don't want to," then fine— just own it. Don't confuse disinterest with inability.

A lot of people are stuck not because they can't, but because they believe they can't. Of course, you can't do something you've never tried, at least not well. Yet, ask a group of kindergartners who can draw, and they'll all raise their hands because no one has told them they can't. By high school, of that same group, only a few will raise their hands because ability becomes a comparison. You don't need to be the best to say you can. Each of my fitness clients is an athlete, yet none will be Olympians. Just like them, until you see yourself as capable with the ability to improve if you want to, you won't be.

I was not born with a library of instruction manuals in my head, but I truly believe that knowledge is power. It gives you the opportunity to talk to people about various topics even if you aren't an expert. Not only can you cross apply knowledge, but you also get a sense of when people are bullshitting you. For example, when quoting you on a house project or while buying a new car.

Maybe you are someone who realizes that they are not naturally curious. If that is true, ask yourself what you always wanted to try but felt you couldn't? Imagine the possibilities if you approached life with the confidence of a kindergartner. You might discover a bit of pride and satisfaction from trying something new and succeeding, even if just a little. Start small and don't be afraid to fail. After all, every mistake is just another step towards success. Now go descale the coffee maker. I bet there is a manual or a video online.

5TH COURSE

Life is a lot like a tasting menu—unpredictable, curated, and full of surprises. Each course brings something new to the table, not always something you would have chosen but something worth trying. Some dishes are exciting, bursting with flavor and possibility, while others make you pause, wondering what exactly you just tasted. It's not about liking every bite; it's about showing up for the experience and trusting that it all adds up to something meaningful in the end.

Think about the first time you ordered a sampler platter. It was probably a mix of mozzarella sticks, chicken wings, and potato skins. A little random, definitely fried, but fun to pick at and share. Early life feels like that, too, doesn't it? A mix of disjointed experiences, messy relationships, and trial-and-error attempts at figuring out who you are. I often joke that is what going away to college is for. You don't realize it at the time, but those random, chaotic bites are laying the foundation for who you become and the version you reject.

As life moves forward, the randomness starts to take shape. The sampler platter turns into small plates, and your choices begin to feel more intentional. You start to select who you want at your table more carefully as you begin to learn that it's not about filling the table with noise or taking up all the space; it's about learning to collaborate as you select your shared plates. The best moments often come from creating something together—whether it's sharing a laugh over dinner, a success, or simply trusting that someone's got your back. Those connections are what turn an ordinary meal into a memorable one.

But connection takes effort. It's not just about showing up; it's about being present and paying attention. It's like keeping your mobile devices off the table. It's about listening as much as you talk, and sometimes, it's about stepping back to let someone else take the lead. Not every person at the table will stay forever, and not every relationship will fit seamlessly. But every interaction offers something—a chance to learn about yourself, to grow, or simply to appreciate the moment.

That's where honesty and authenticity come in. With every person I have the privilege of interacting with, I remind them that whoever they are is totally fine. And if they don't like that version then it is up to them to change. But first, they must be honest with themselves about what they want, what they're willing to give, and what they need to let go of. The same goes for being honest with others. It's not always easy, but clarity wins every time. Sometimes that means acknowledging when something isn't working and having the courage to move on. Not every plate needs to be cleaned, and not every dish is worth finishing.

At some point, you've probably heard that you need to trust the process. That means trusting yourself to handle the unexpected and trusting the people you've invited to your table. It's not blind faith; it's a willingness to show up and engage with what's in front of you, even when it feels uncertain. Trust is what lets you take the next step, the next bite, the next risk.

The truth is, not every moment will feel profound or life-changing, and that's okay. Some courses are bold and memorable, while others are quiet and unassuming. But each one plays its part, adding its memory to your life. *It's not about perfection; it's about participation.* It's about the energy you bring, the effort you make, and the risks you're willing to take. Because in the end, what we get out of life is shaped by how much we're willing to show up and engage and is often a reflection of what we're willing to give.

Diversity

When I look around today, I can't help but notice the growing tendency for different groups to feel the need to push their way to the front. I used to think the goal was for everyone, no matter their background, to coexist peacefully. I thought it was about finding common ground, not about power struggles or seeing who could be the loudest. But now, it feels like we're stuck in a cycle where each group feels like it's their turn to dominate the conversation.

In the desire to feel loved, welcomed, and seen, I've noticed some minority groups adopting an "it's my turn now" mentality. And while I understand the need to be heard and valued—don't we all?—I believe this approach often leads to conflict rather than resolution. I always thought the goal was to share the room, not take it over. This is where I believe we've gone off course.

I had a conversation with my friend James, who works at a major financial institution. He's an older white man, and we were talking about his company's diversity and inclusion programs. James explained that the programs offered support to women and other minorities. While James was in full support of elevating minority groups, here's where it went sideways for him: During a national conference, two women talked about how inclusive the company had become, especially for women, but then they said, "Now it's time for us to take over." That's where James got lost, and I don't blame him. He felt threatened, not by diversity, but by the notion that sharing the room wasn't enough, now it had to be taken over. Language matters, and whether their words echoed a genuine need for dominance or was a poorly worded speech, it was off-putting for many.

James wasn't opposed to sharing; he just didn't want to feel displaced. This is something I think a lot of people feel, especially those in traditionally powerful positions. It's not about resisting progress; it's about not wanting to be pushed out. I see this in many areas, whether it's race, gender, or religion.

Recently, I attended a women's business conference where two Black female panelists said something that really resonated with me. They spoke about the importance of embracing men as advocates rather than seeing them as the enemy. They shared how, for them, it was a man who had provided the best mentorship, advocacy, and support throughout their careers. What would change if we saw more men as allies in the fight for female equality, rather than as obstacles? This mindset of collaboration rather than confrontation was so refreshing to hear. It's not about taking over the room or pitting one group against another. It's about working together to create space for everyone.

James' experience made me think about how easily a well-intentioned conversation can turn divisive. We need to recognize that most people aren't looking to overthrow anything, they just want a seat at the table, not the entire room.

Disconnected Connection

Technology is incredible. It's brought the world to our fingertips, but it's also created a separation that's harder to see. This isn't a physical divide, but one that feels even more profound to me—an emotional and figurative distance. It's like eating dinner at the same table, but everyone's staring at their mobile device. Together, but separate.

It is a divide that allows people to hide behind hard discussions, instead opting for "break up" texts, while also creating misunderstandings—a result of the lack of tone, context, and that intangible thing we call non-verbal communication. As a coach, I will always opt for in-person sessions versus virtual ones; something my clients prefer also, with virtual as a last resort.

We say things like, "We should get together soon," but how often do we pull out our calendars and actually make it happen? When someone tells me that, I usually throw out some dates right then. Sometimes they are confused by the idea of planning in the moment, other times they think it's a great thing to do. If you want to see someone, if you truly want to connect, don't wait. Schedule it. Don't let "We should get together soon" be your default goodbye. Make it real. And if you don't genuinely want to get together, don't throw it out there as an empty offer. Why say it if you don't mean it?

Despite the often daily virtual interactions people had during the Covid-19 pandemic, many found themselves longing for the presence of others, even if it was just a select few. The isolation highlighted the balance we all need: time alone to recharge and time with others to feel connected. Even introverts who need solitude to recharge, still need connection.

I heard many clients during the early days of the pandemic lockdown profess their joy over never leaving their house, proudly waving their banner of introversion. Fast forward one month and they were ready to see friends and colleagues face to face again, if only a little bit. I reminded them that even introverts like people, it's just they prefer people who don't upset their peace. On the other hand, extroverts who thrive among people and feed off collective energy, longed for group interaction, often falling into a depressive state. The pandemic showed us just how much we all rely on each other, no matter where we fall on the introvert-extrovert spectrum. Sometimes, connection is less about feasting and more about those small, shared bites that keep us grounded in each other's lives.

Neuroscientist Matthew Lieberman writes in his book, *Social: Why Our Brains Are Wired to Connect,* that our modern brains are literally wired to reach out and connect with others. But that doesn't mean we don't need time alone. If you find yourself feeling irritable, overwhelmed, or anxious after too much social interaction, it's often a sign that you need to take a step back. Alone time gives you the chance to break free from social pressures and tap into your own thoughts, feelings, and experiences.

While connection is important, I am not denying the importance of solitude which fosters creativity. When you're not distracted by the noise of the world, your mind has the space to wander, to dream, to create. As a self-professed social introvert, my best time of reflection is when I'm mowing the lawn or painting that delicate line between the wall and the ceiling. Alone. In silence.

The energy you get when you are physically around others can turn a good conversation into a great one, or a simple get-together into something memorable. But with screens between us, that energy is missing. And it's not just with the small things like texting. I've heard from friends who walk into their kids' rooms only to find them alone, sitting at a computer, headphones on, hanging out in a virtual world with friends who live only blocks away. The tools that were meant to supplement our connections have instead become the norm in many cases.

It's easy to blame technology for the distance we feel at times, but it's also important to recognize its role in keeping us connected. After all, without technology, many of us would lose touch with friends and family who live far away. It's a tool, a powerful one, but like any tool, it's all in how you use it.

Technology can connect us to people we've never met, people who live on the other side of the world. It can bring us closer to those who share our passions, our interests, our goals. But it can also create a false sense of connection, one that leaves us feeling empty rather than fulfilled, like foraging for a meal from a vending machine.

Gone are the days of kids showing up at your door asking if your son or daughter could come out to play. Or teenagers hanging out at a mall, park, or another social destination. The key to using technology for connection is to use it mindfully. Don't let it replace the real, tangible interactions in your life. Instead, let it enhance them. Use it to stay in touch, to share moments, to keep relationships alive when distance makes it difficult. But don't let it be a substitute for the energy, the warmth, the humanity that comes from being truly present with someone. Use it to arrange time with other people, even if only a phone call.

With all the forms of technology available to us, what keeps us from reaching out when someone pops into our minds? Is it fear of rejection? Is it busyness or does it feel like another chore on a never-ending list? Are we too concerned they'll wonder if there is other motivation for reaching out?

Next time someone comes to mind consider sending them a quick text, an email, or even—imagine this—making a phone call. Just to say "hi." Just to check in. You'd be surprised how much it means to someone to hear from you, even if it's just a few words. And in doing so, you bring yourself back to the present. Connection isn't just a word; it's an action, and it doesn't need to be time-consuming. It's the tiny tether that says, "You came into my mind."

How Was School?

One of my clients, Tom, was having a hard time with his teenage son. He told me, "I want to understand him, but I don't even know where to start." Tom's a business guy. He's structured, logical, used to solving problems with steps and strategy. But that approach wasn't getting him anywhere at home.

I said, "What if you tried getting to know him the same way you get to know a new company or client? You ask questions, you listen, you figure out what's going on behind the scenes. You don't start by fixing, you start by learning." Then I added, half-joking, "Or just say something that makes him roll his eyes. If he's rolling his eyes, he's at least he's listening."

So he tried it.

Instead of the usual "How was school?" or "Did you do your homework?"—which always got a one-word answer—he asked his son to show him some music he liked. His son stared at him like, *why are you trying?* With a little nudging from Tom, he played a couple songs. Then Tom played him a few from when he was a teenager. His son hated them, which opened the door for a little back-and-forth. They didn't get deep, but they started talking more. And then a little more.

Over the next few weeks, things shifted a bit and the tension softened. Tom told me the conversations didn't feel so forced; they were finding a rhythm. That's when I reminded him that connection isn't something that responds to force; it responds to presence. He didn't have to be cool or say the right thing. He just needed to care enough to keep showing up, and let his son meet him halfway at his own pace.

Sometimes connection brews slowly. And sometimes, it's trial and error like trying a new recipe. What matters most is that you stay in the kitchen—tweaking the seasoning, adjusting the timing, and hoping the next version is better than the last.

F*@k Gail!

We all have triggers. One of mine? Headline readers. People who grab onto emotionally charged claims, skim a video snippet, or read a clickbait title and suddenly have a strong opinion on something they barely understand. I don't say that to be critical; I say it because I've seen its impact up close. Whether it's politics or nutrition, there's a version out there to fit every belief.

One of my fitness clients, Steve, had struggled with his relationship with food and resulting obesity for decades. One day, he came in and told me his friend Gail had given him some nutrition tips. Now, in general, I think sharing good information is great. But I knew Gail. Steve had mentioned her often, and I knew she had her own long-standing struggles with wellness.

"So, Gail said I shouldn't be eating carbs," he told me. "Just protein. And only eat twice a day."

I blinked. "Gail? The friend who's also been battling her health for years?"

"Yeah."

"Where did she get this?"

"She saw something online."

We had been over this. More than once. And I could feel my patience thinning.

"F*@k Gail," I said.

He raised his eyebrows. I paused. "Steve, I know you're frustrated. I know you're desperate for something that feels simple and doable. But no matter who said what, this comes down to you—your mindset, your choices, and your willingness to change your habits. That includes buying real food. Preparing it. Fueling your body in a way that supports you."

"I know," he said. "I just wish it didn't feel so hard."

This wasn't just about Steve or Gail. It's about how easily we grab onto anything that sounds like a solution. A podcast soundbite. A friend's routine. A comment about a photo that captures one second of a much bigger story. When you're tired, overwhelmed, or just want something to work, those fragments can feel like they must be right.

But most of what gets shared today, especially in media and wellness spaces, are designed to provoke a reaction, not offer clarity. Bold promises. Easy fixes. A headline that reinforces what we already believe or fear. And when we stop at the headline or repeat something we barely remember hearing, we're not helping each other. We're spreading confusion.

I asked Steve if he remembered what carbohydrates are.

"Bread?" he offered.

"Yes. But also fruit. Vegetables. Beans. Lentils. *Carbs aren't the problem. Being unprepared is.*" And so is the way we consume information in pieces without understanding the full picture.

That's the risk of cherry-picking advice or letting someone else do it for you. You lose the context. And context matters.

We're living in a world built around fast answers and quick rewards. But the kind of change that actually lasts comes from slowing down. From learning. From being curious enough to ask better questions, even when it's inconvenient or uncomfortable. That's how we stop being reactive and start being intentional. It's how we have more grounded conversations about politics, nutrition, and everything in between.

You don't have to research everything or know all the answers. But if something matters to you—your health, your future, your vote—take the time to learn more than the headline. Read the whole article. Listen to the entire conversation. Compare a few differing sources.

Sometimes the most powerful thing you can do is admit that you don't know. And then go find out. You deserve better than emotionally charged soundbites and oversimplified advice. You don't need to eat the whole buffet; but please don't build your plate based on what Gail said was good last Tuesday.

Effort

I began my fitness career at a big box gym. I remember one occasion noticing a young woman sitting on a piece of strength training equipment as if her connection to the seat would create the change she wanted. She caught my attention because she had been there for quite a while, moving her arms here and there with barely any effort and long pauses in between each pair of repetitions.

"What are you working on today?" I asked. "Not sure, I just go to whatever machine is open and do some reps," she shrugged.

That was it. She was there, roaming the gym, barely putting in any effort.

I knew she had effectively created a habit of going to the gym because I saw her frequently, but it was like she expected that her habit of passing through the door was enough to help her reach her goals. Like so many people, she believed that just physically showing up was all she needed to do. Whether it's about business, learning something new, or taking care of your body, you must do more than just show up. *Showing up isn't just about being physically present; it's about being focused, on-point, and truly engaged.*

Have you ever signed up for a course and didn't follow through? Bought a fitness program and barely participated? You're not alone. I've been there, too.

My years coaching people in various formats has taught me a number of lessons, but the most prevalent one is that *most people want change*, but

- Don't want to put in the effort required to create change.
- Don't want to change anything about their current effort; or,
- Don't find an effective process, resource or tool to model that will lead to positive change.

So, what I do is help people sort through what they really want versus what they think they should want. A lot of the things people want to achieve are leftovers, routines and habits from long ago that may no longer suit them. Once that new perspective is revealed they need to uncover and implement the positive strategies needed to achieve their goals—which can be anything from improving their relationships or wellness and mental health, to finding new and effective ways to make a better impact at work or home.

When I became a part-time adjunct professor of business for one semester, I remember thinking it was like karma because, although I was not a fan of reading textbooks as a student, I always knew that when I did read, I got more out of it. Instead, as a student I was very focused on attending the lectures, which seemed to have been enough for me to get at least a B average.

What I knew from my experience was that students needed to be engaged in multiple ways to succeed just as I did when I was younger. In addition to the lectures, I encouraged my students to actively participate by reading the textbook and teaching a section in small group format to get them involved. I didn't realize at the time that I was making them utilize all the modalities of learning I use as a growth coach—reading, listening and speaking, analyzing, and hands-on activities.

My methods very directly forced the students to be engaged. But here's the thing: you must go to class. I remember one student, Teon, looking at me in the middle of class and blurting out, "Am I gonna pass this class?" I looked at him quizzically and said, "Well, this isn't an appropriate discussion right now. But let me ask you this: do you think you're gonna pass this class considering you only show up half the time, and you haven't turned in most of your homework?"

I told him later during a break that if he was interested in passing this class, he needed to show up and participate fully. He paused, looked at me, and said, "You know, Miss Nicole, you're a little scary, but you keep it real." I laughed and told him I could only guide him, but if he showed up to class and put in the effort, he would pass. Though he wasn't the best student, he passed the class with a C. For a student who often failed his classes that was pretty remarkable.

Goal setting is not just about showing up but putting in the effort to achieve those goals. Too often, people are not taught the strategies necessary to do this.

On another occasion, I was working with a fitness client who was half-heartedly punching and kicking a bag. I asked him to please put in some real effort. He looked back at me with a sigh, citing that he didn't think he got anything out of the exercise, and it was dumb. So, I explained the reason for the activity: it was a cardiovascular challenge, and it also worked on his shoulders and hip flexors. But none of that would be true if he didn't put forth the effort to make it so. He rolled his eyes a little bit but then proceeded to do it with energy and effort. When he finished, he looked at me winded and said, "Oh, I get it now."

What I'm trying to illustrate here is that you must do more than just show up; you must put forth effort. If you're unwilling, ask yourself if it is really that important to you. Do you think you'll fail anyway, or are you just satisfying a "should do" from your list?

Can you imagine the difference it would make if you were truly engaged with your goals? What if you poured your energy and effort into your endeavors, rather than just doing the bare minimum? Think about what you could achieve if you went beyond being physically present. Don't settle for "at least I tried." Did you really try? Did you put in the effort? Did you push yourself? Imagine the possibilities if you did.

You get out what you put in. So, if you're just going through the motions, don't be surprised if you don't achieve your goals. But if you put in the effort, if you're truly engaged and committed, you can achieve so much more than you ever thought possible.

Dance Floor

High school dances were a weird mix of wanting to be social but also wanting to sit on the bleachers. Maybe you were the one who treated school dances like a dance show audition. Or maybe you were like me, moving enough to blend in, but never really going for it like I did while blaring music and dancing alone in my bedroom.

When the slow songs came on, I was good. I could sway and rock back and forth like every other duo. But the upbeat songs? Forget it. I'd start out moving, but then the music would get faster, and my body would want to do more than a rhythmic bounce and sway, but I knew I would look silly if I joined in. So instead of letting loose, back to the bleacher's edge I would go to fabricate needing a break or make conversation.

Then one night at the high school gymnasium it finally happened; I got brave. I don't remember if it was a homecoming or a Valentine's dance, but I finally decided to join my friends in our little dance pod with more than a sway, as in letting my body move as though it felt all the music. Moments after joining our little circle my exuberant friend Paige saw me, her eyes and body language lighting up as she announced, "Oh my gosh, you're dancing!" I swear, the room went silent and suddenly I was the center of attention. At least that is what my mind told me. Despite my horror, I did my best to push through but reverted to the "sway" and eventually to the sidelines.

Paige was just trying to be supportive. I knew that intellectually, but it wasn't what I needed at that moment. I didn't need a spotlight on me. I just wanted to get comfortable, maybe move a little without feeling like the whole world was watching me.

That moment made me realize how important it is to meet people where they are when they're trying something new, especially if it makes them uncomfortable. Sometimes supporting people is about creating space for them to take baby steps. It's offering them a taste of your meal rather than forcing them to eat the whole dish. It's the small, subtle gestures that make them feel safe, like a nod or a smile to say, "I see you and you are okay," rather than a loud cheer. That's the kind of support that makes it easier for someone to try again, and maybe next time, they'll dance just a little more confidently.

CHECK, PLEASE

Our collective journeys boil down to one thing: showing up and honoring where you are. For yourself, for others, and for the life you're still building. It's about being bold enough to try something new, knowing it's just one bite. It's about appreciating the simplicity of grilled cheese while savoring the complexities of a tasting menu. It's about finding the courage to step into the unknown and the grace to honor where you've been.

So, what's your grilled cheese? The thing that brings you comfort when life feels overwhelming. And what's your tasting menu—the thing that challenges you to grow, to stretch, to see yourself in a new way? Wherever you are on your journey, know this: You're allowed to grow. You're allowed to evolve. And you're allowed to find joy in the messiness of it all.

Because at the end of the day, life isn't about choosing between grilled cheese and tasting menus. It's about embracing both. It's about knowing when to lean into comfort and when to step into curiosity. It's about savoring every bite, no matter how familiar or unfamiliar, and trusting that each one is part of your story.

GRILLED CHEESE MENU

Grilled cheese is one of my favorite comfort foods. When I was a kid and I wasn't feeling well, my mom would make me grilled cheese cut into quarters. As I've gotten older, grilled cheese is still my go-to comfort food when I'm sick (and especially when it is cold outside and I can't seem to warm up). I don't like anything fancy—just basic white bread, American cheese, and mayo on the outside of the bread to crisp it up. Of course, I still cut it up into quarters.

Lauren N. — Hickory, NC

One of the best ways to get yourself back in working order after a night of too many drinks is a grilled cheese with bacon and tomato. A little crunchy and a bit gooey. Mmmm!

Heather C. — Pompano Beach, FL

Authentic Dutch Edam cheese on fresh, buttered bread sprinkled with white pepper, then grilled. It's soooo tasty!

Kim V. — Albury, NSW, Australia

I like to take sourdough bread, spread one side with butter and one with pesto, and grill it with the butter side down. Add your choice of quality cheese (mozzarella, provolone, sharp cheddar). Pair with tomato basil soup. Mmmmmm good! When I was a kid I used Velveeta or American.

Cathy F. — Punta Gorda, FL

Growing up in South America we didn't have central heating, so we kept a log fire burning in the fireplace pretty much the entire winter. Some days after school, my brothers and I would make "sandwiches calientes" on handheld iron sandwich makers. Two slices of "American" bread, butter, Swiss cheese, and a couple slices of ham. Then we'd stand by the fireplace holding the sandwich maker's long handle, flipping it over the flames while we talked stories and sipped hot chocolate. Those were the days.

Laura G. — Pompano Beach, FL

I love grilled cheese and would have one every day if I could. I love it paired with tomato soup, and I often make it for my kids when we need a quick, warm, and delicious meal. My mom used to add tomato slices and called it "greasy cheesy with tomato." I like using rye, sourdough, or Italian bread, filled with a mix of sharp cheddar, Swiss, and even a layer of cream cheese. I also add mustard or tomato for a little bit of "zing."

Courtney Z. — Silver Lake, OH

I love cutting my grilled cheese into cubes and adding them as croutons to a bowl of tomato soup!

Azmeena D. — Chicago, IL

The thought of grilled cheese brings back memories of gooey provolone and Swiss cheese seeping out the sides and my mom cutting it into triangles and serving it with tomato soup. Grilled cheese is like a giant hug from my childhood. Everyone in my home now likes a different cheese combo.

Karen C. — Streetsboro, OH

I start my grilled cheese by evenly buttering two slices of artesano brioche bread. Next, I sprinkle both slices with a healthy amount of garlic powder, Italian seasoning, and just a pinch of onion powder. One slice goes in the pan, seasoned side down, topped with a slice of white American cheese. Then, I top it with the other slice of bread to seal my grilled cheese!

Emma K. — Davie, FL

A firehouse favorite is sourdough bread, melted Swiss cheese, pulled pork, and pickles with BBQ sauce grilled in a cast iron skillet with butter.

BBQ sauce ingredients: cane sugar, tomato paste, brown sugar, paprika, Dijon mustard, Worcestershire sauce, sea salt, ground pepper, and minced garlic.

Raleigh Z. — Melrose, FL

The ultimate grilled cheese starts with homemade brioche sourdough. A mix of creamy goat cheese and fontina, with the addition of fig preserves hits all the right notes. Kerrygold salted Irish butter provides that perfect texture when creating this comforting sandwich. I have fond memories of eating grilled cheese, especially on a cold, winter day.

Jenne C. — Bay Village, OH

Grilled cheese is the go-to when there is nothing else in the fridge because those are the two food staples I always have: cheese and bread. When I was little my mom would make grilled cheese with white Wonder bread, margarine, and Kraft singles. Today my favorite is sourdough or pumpernickel bread with a bit of avocado oil and Gouda cheese. Nothing quite like it.

Mae W. — Oakland Park, FL

My all-time favorite grilled cheese is white bread with two types of any cheese, butter...and the banger—caramelized onions. Omg, knocks me out every time. I can't get enough.

Bandi M. — Jacksonville Beach, FL

I take thick multigrain bread, melt butter in a skillet, move the bread around to soak it in, and lay white American cheese on top so it starts to melt. When it's about halfway done, I take the bread out, scramble a couple of eggs, add them to the sandwich, and grill it until it's perfectly browned.

Erin C. — Fort Lauderdale, FL

You really can't screw up a grilled cheese. I use all kinds of cheeses: Gruyère because it melts well; Wisconsin cheddar for sharp taste; or something soft like a French Brie or Italian spreadable goat for the "perfect" weight. I like to mix it up and try new things. It's just a sandwich so you can't be afraid to get it wrong.

Alex C. — Greenville, SC

ACKNOWLEDGEMENTS

To my wife Jeana: For always supporting my life journey, including my clumsiness and injuries.

To my book coach Cathy Fyock: Thank you for trusting my process and guiding me on its path.

To my editorial team of Beth, Erin, Melinda, Natalia, and Yoland: Thank you for keeping my stream of thought writing on its path. I appreciated every "I love this" as well each comment that sometimes had me rewriting or deleting stories.

To my dear friend Lori Pratico: My deepest gratitude for sharing your artistic talent and designing the cover.

And to my community of peers: Thank you for contributing nostalgic grilled cheese recipes, sharing those you love today, and for being part of the cover design process once again.

ABOUT THE AUTHOR

Nicole Hollar is a mindset and growth coach, speaker and author. Her bestselling book, *Feeling Stuck? Empower Yourself to Live a Happier, More Fulfilling Life,* is modeled after one of her private coaching programs and guides readers through the 10 Tenets of Mindset Transformation Coaching®; while her workplace leadership guide *Logged In, Checked Out* is an effective tool for enhancing workplace communication and productivity.

In addition to private coaching and writing, Nicole hosts workshops and events, and speaks at private and public conferences and organizations. She tailors each engagement to her audience.

Nicole is board certified by the Association for Integrative Psychology in Mental and Emotional Release® (MER), Neuro-Linguistic Programming (NLP) and Hypnotherapy, the American Council on Exercise, and the OSHAcademy.

Her favorite grilled cheese is:

White or wheat with gooey cheddar, pan-grilled to a light brown crisp with real butter.

For a list of *Grilled Cheese & Tasting Menus: Stories of Growth and Change* **Book Club Conversation Starters,** visit:

www.nicolehollar.com/grilled-cheese

To book Nicole for **Keynotes, Workshops,** or **Development Training,** visit:
www.nicolehollar.com/book-nicole

To learn more about **Mindset Transformation Coaching®** and find other useful other resources visit: www.nicolehollar.com

BOOKS

FEELING STUCK?

Empower Yourself to Live a Happier, More Fulfilling Life

LOGGED IN, CHECKED OUT

Boost Productivity and Improve Communication

FOLLOW NICOLE

@nicolehollarcoaching

Find The *OWN IT* Podcast on Spotify & Apple Podcasts